The Last Six Months

Documented By

Joanna Slater

I Dedicate The Last Six Months To My Beautiful Mother Kay

Contents

Introduction		7
Chapter 1	The day before	9
Chapter 2	One month in hospital	23
Chapter 3	Two months in hospital	31
Chapter 4	Three months in hospital	39
Chapter 5	Four months in hospital	63
Chapter 6	Five months in hospital	82
Chapter 7	Six months in hospital	96
Chapter 8	Conclusion	101
Epilogue	A message from Joanna	105

THE LAST SIX MONTHS

Introduction

I first started to write these notes purely as a reminder of all the things that happened to my mother soon throughout the first few weeks when she arrived in hospital for a routine hip operation. As things started going wrong with my mother's health so soon after her operation I was advised by my manager Paul at work to start making notes. What a good idea!

Each day before I started work I would enter onto my computer all my notes from the previous day. I would never have thought I would still be writing six months later. My notes have become an up-to-date diary of my mother and how her condition deteriorated during this terrible and tragic course of events. It has also allowed me to capture all the memories of our time together while she was in hospital: the laughs, the tears, the precious words that were spoken and how lucky am I to have captured it all.

I have two sisters both of whom underwent their own personal traumas; all of us suffered emotionally during our mother's stay in hospital. I have not mentioned my sister's names as I did not want it to look as if one was at the hospital caring more than the other as this was not the case. All three of us did as much as we could and would have done more if we could of.

But these are *my* notes, my own personal account of my

thoughts and feelings and I want my story to be brought to the members of the public as this is still happening in our hospitals today and we should always be aware to write everything down because it's so easy to forget.

It had taken me three years to make my diary public which I first put on a blog, three years to go back on my notes filling in all the details which has brought back the hurt and pain my mother went through.

I have had to change the names of people for legal reasons.
Thank you for reading The Last Six Months, I hope it will open up your eyes and your hearts.

Joanna

CHAPTER ONE

The Day Before

18th July 2007: One beautiful warm summer evening Mum took my two sisters and me out for dinner as she was going into hospital the following day for her hip operation. She had her favorite meal, minted lamb and roast potatoes with a glass of white wine, and was talking and laughing about how she would be able to run the marathon after her operation. She added that she was looking forward to being able to do all the things she used to do such as driving her car, going shopping and just being independent. Oh, how she hated having to rely on anyone! We had such a lovely time that night, unaware that this would be the last meal all four of us would have together.

My father Eddie died 13 years ago but mum was always a very independent lady. She had worked in retail sales all her life up until her early 70s and always took pride in her appearance. Smart, well groomed, attractive and even now at the age of 84 looked a good 10 years younger.
She always loved working but eventually had to stop because of her age, this was something which greatly upset her.

Mum had been in pain for about 18 months with her hip so she hardly went out anymore. She had a hip replacement operation nearly 20 years ago but she is now having problems again. In a hip replacement operation the damaged ball and socket are removed and they are replaced with an artificial ball and socket made of metal, plastic or ceramic. They say that hip replacements wear out eventually over a period of about 10 - 20 years.

Basically the ball now keeps on coming out of its socket and it has to be replaced. So mum will be having revision hip replacement surgery.

Every Saturday I used to take mum out shopping until she found it too painful to walk. Mum was also very frightened to walk in case she fell over as she had done so many times before.
I remember one day she had fallen down at her home, unfortunately she had refused to wear the personal alarm which I had arranged for her and she had been on the floor for hours on her own until I arrived after phoning her with no answer. She had locked the door from the inside with a chain so my son Paul had to break the door down. Oh how she wanted to get her independence back.

In Hospital

19th July: I took the day off work with the intention of driving mum to the hospital and arrived at her home about 10 in the morning. She had already packed her bag and had made sure that her home was looking spick and span as she would never leave it in a mess. Mum was quite nervous at the thought of the operation but she had undergone operations in the past and knew what to expect. She was not frightened of hospitals as unfortunately my father had been quite an ill man all through their married life. Mum had been used to going back and forth to hospitals over the years to visit him when he was not well. She learnt to drive when my sisters and I were very small which made it easier for her to travel to and from the hospital with us.

We arrived at the hospital about midday and made our way to the Orthopaedics Ward which looked quite dismal. The nurse came over to mum and asked her to get undressed and pop onto bed to wait for

her consultant Mr Shah to arrive. We did not have to wait long for him to arrive and after introducing himself to me he went through the procedure of the operation.
Mum smiled and said, "I know I am in good hands."

The Hip Operation

20th July: Mum's hip operation was done today. Thank goodness it's over. I could not wait till 5.30 when I finish at work to go and see mum as I work full time.
When my sisters and I arrived at the hospital mum was quite sleepy but seemed in good spirits. She told us that she had an x-ray soon after the operation and the doctors had been very pleased with how the operation had gone. The next days that followed mum's progress seems quite slow and really not much news to report.

Physiotherapy starting

23rd July: Mum is being given physiotherapy but she seems to be in a lot pain and now she is getting quite frustrated at her slow progress. My sisters and I make sure that we see her every day after work and bring her food and bottled water. Mum does not like the food in the hospital, nor would I, it reminds me of school dinners but that's going back years and years ago. She has her mobile phone thank goodness so we speak often in the day, when I arrive I charge the phone so she can always be in contact with us.

Quite concerned

28th July: Thank goodness it's Saturday, at least we won't have to rush from work and we can be with mum all day. When I ask the nurses how mum is they say she is fine but I am becoming quite concerned as she doesn't seem to be improving so I will speak to the doctor's after the weekend. Mum is speaking to the other patients in the ward so at least it's not too boring for her, but the magazines and books we have brought she has not looked at, she said she cannot put her mind on them.

In Pain

1st August: Mum has now been in hospital for just under two weeks. My manager Paul at work has suggested I write regularly in a diary so I can keep a check on how she is progressing each day. What a good idea.
I am very concerned as mum is being given physiotherapy regularly but she is in constant pain and cannot walk yet so she is being given painkillers, mum also seems quite breathless. I will speak to her consultant tomorrow.

Spoken to the consultant

2nd August: I have spoken to Mum's consultant and told him how worried my sisters and I are about mum's progress. I asked him why is she still in so much pain nearly two weeks after her operation. Surely she should be up and walking around. He did not have any answers for me and said that she was due to have a second x-ray this evening so we shall see what it reveals.

Bad News

3rd August: I have spoken to Mr Shah but bad news, Mum results from the second x-ray shows that her hip is dislocated. Oh my goodness, how can that be! Poor mum, no wonder why she has been in so much pain. I feel so bad, why the hell didn't I speak up earlier. Here she is in hospital with qualified doctors and nurses who should know that there is a problem with mum; I am not getting a very good feeling about this.

Mum has not been out of bed since her operation apart from when she had physiotherapy, could the physiotherapy have caused the hip to dislocate? Mr Shah says that mum will have to undergo another operation to have her hip put back in place.

He said that the reason mum has been quite breathless is that she now has a problem with her kidneys. An examination has shown that this is possibly due to the drugs, pain killers, etc she had been given for the pain. What on earth is going wrong? Mum has never had a problem with her kidneys before, not that I am aware of. Apparently she needs to be given more fluid so her kidneys can function correctly before the second operation can take place under a general anaesthetic. This is now booked for 10th August and will allow time for Mum's kidneys to start to work properly again. Not surprisingly, mum is getting very frustrated but I'm trying to make light of the situation so as not to worry her, but my mother is not stupid.

Helpless

4th August: It's the weekend and when we arrive at the hospital we are shocked to see that Mum is on an intravenous saline drip. A saline drip is used to rehydrate the body when the body is dehydrated to improve or restore body function. It is administered via a tube using an injection needle which is put directly into the vein. She is becoming very anxious and we are trying to keep her spirits up but she is clearly worried. I'm finding it hard to know what to say to her and trying to find a doctor to talk to is a joke. I eventually speak to Dr Mehra one of the registrars on duty. He says the saline drip has been given to Mum as she needs more fluid for her kidneys, how helpless we feel.

Shocked

5th August: Mum has been breathless again today and now is on an oxygen mask but off the saline drip. The nurse tells me that apparently too much fluid has been given to her which has resulted in mum being breathless. Why was too much fluid given to her? I want to see a doctor but its Sunday and you cannot find anyone to talk to on a Sunday.

Darren and Paul (my two sons) have come to see their grandma but she looks really awful. They are very close to their grandma and shocked to see her this way, I don't know quite what to say to them. They are trying not to show how shocked they are by trying to humour mum but she can see through them and not saying much.

Very down

6th August: The start of a new week and I arrive at the hospital around 6.30 having come straight from work. Mum is very down and getting very angry, she is now having drugs to relieve the excess fluid from her kidneys. She tells me that she had another chest x-ray today but did not really want to talk that much again. I chatted to the patient in the bed opposite mum and she said that she thought mum was a bit confused and disorientated which is worrying. My sisters came and we all stayed till about 8 o'clock then left to go home.

Saline drip

7th August: I arrived tonight at the hospital to find Mum on the saline drip again. I sat down next to mum's bed when a female doctor about 35 ish with blond hair approached mum's bed. She introduced herself as Dr Field who is from the Renal (kidney department). She was furious when she sees a saline drip has been given to mum again. Apparently, the drip should have come off of mum's notes but it was still there. Doctor Field takes mum off the drip straight away but mum is now so breathless due to the excess fluid which has been given to her that the nurses have to put her on an oxygen mask again.
Dr Field tells me that my mother may have to go on to a dialysis machine to get her kidneys working properly again.
Nearly three weeks in hospital and mum is worse than when she went in. Not only she cannot walk yet but she also has problems with her kidneys now.
You can never see a doctor when you visit unless you hang around in the morning and try to catch them on their rounds. That is impossible when you're working but I have arranged for my sisters and me to have a meeting with one of the ward doctors at 9am tomorrow to

discuss Mum's condition then we can go to work later.

I have so many questions to ask. How could Mum's hip become dislocated days after the operation leaving her unable to walk? It also seems that the pain started after the first time the physiotherapist came to work on mum, could that have been the cause of her hip dislocating?

Why did mum have to wait so long for a second x-ray nearly two weeks after her operation when she was clearly in so much pain? The doctors knew she was in pain and that's why they gave her painkillers. Was the correct procedure given to mum before she went into hospital?

Had she been examined to ensure she was fit and well enough to have a general anaesthetic? Why was the saline drip still on mum's medical notes when they knew that she had too much fluid?

Going round in circles

8th August: It's 9am and with all my notes written down we go in to see a doctor called Dr Mehra. But when I asked him all my questions we have he seems to be going round in circles and not giving me any straight answers, oh surprise, surprise. So I demand to speak with Mr Shah my mother's consultant. He arranged the meeting for 1.30 this afternoon, so my sisters and I will not go back to work.

It's 1 o'clock and we go into the meeting with Mr Shah. He cannot give us an answer as to why mum's hip has dislocated as he just does not know. He doesn't comment why mum waited so long for a second x-ray and he says he did explain to mum before she went into hospital all the things that can go wrong when you have surgery. But that's as much as he'll tell us, he hopes to give mum the operation on Friday 10th August to manipulate her hip back as long as her kidneys get the

go ahead. Meeting with him seems to have been a waste of time, you think you know what they are saying but when you try and remember the conversation you're even more confused.
We also spoke to Dr Field while we were at the hospital and she said that she would like to put a temporary port (dialysis catheter) which would be inserted into a vein just below mum's collar bone today so she'll be ready to have her dialysis for the operation on Friday. This allows blood to flow out of the body and another opening (port) for blood to return back into the body after it flows through the dialysis machine.
We then went into see mum for a little while, she was happy but surprised to see us so early and asked why? We said that we wanted to speak to her doctors for them to explain to us the next procedure for her hip, and also we explained to her about the dialysis which is only temporary until her kidneys start working better again. She was pleased that we had explained it to her; we stayed a while then went home.

I'm home now, its quarter to 4 and I've just received a phone call from the sister of the orthopaedics ward to tell me about mum's dialysis. The port may not now be inserted into mum today as the room may not be available so it may be tomorrow. As I put the phone down I thought "what room"
We all went back to see mum this evening and find her breathless and stressed. The nurse will put an oxygen mask back on her to help with her breathing. It's really hard knowing what to say and we don't want to worry her, we asked mum if she would like to watch the TV. Each bed has a small screen attached to a bracket which swivels round from the wall. You have to pay for it but that's not a problem as long as it alleviates mum's boredom. However, she has no interest in it; she must feel bad as she doesn't even have the patience to watch her beloved Eastenders.

Sore

9th August: Tonight, thank goodness, Mum is not so breathless, although now we find out that she is on a strong antibiotic, the result of a sore on her leg from the medical stockings she has to wear. The sore has been there for some time since her hip operation but we didn't know about it and our mum bless her does not really complain. The doctors tell us that it wasn't necessary to put Mum on the dialysis machine today; they say they will put the port in tomorrow while she is under the general anaesthetic having her operation.

2nd Operation

10th August: Mum went down to the operating theatre today to have her hip manoeuvred back into place. I phoned the hospital ward to ask how she was and according to the doctors the operation went well (fingers crossed). They are very pleased with her and she is now back on the ward but very drowsy from the anaesthetic and still in pain so she's being given liquid morphine intravenously to help with the pain. The renal doctor, Dr Field came to see mum about 3 o'clock and told us that mum would start to have dialysis tomorrow and the port has been inserted.
Let's hope that this is now the turning point and mum can start to get better, walk and come home.

A phone call

11th August: It's Saturday morning at 8 and my home phone is ringing. it's a call from the night nurse in the orthopaedic ward to say Mum's kidneys are not functioning properly. Apparently she was breathless in the night and was put on an oxygen mask. She also has bad pains in her back and had been seen by many doctors throughout the night. Yet again she has been given drugs to release the fluid from her kidneys. She must be pretty bad if the nurse decided to phone me so early in the morning. Mum will be going for dialysis today, I'm certainly very worried.

My sisters and I arrived at the hospital early today and mum looked really ill and breathless. She was in a deep sleep and still has an oxygen mask on her face. About quarter past two the nurse came in and asked us to stand outside while she redressed the sore on mum's leg. We stood outside while she pulled the curtains and we could hear mum had woken up as she was obviously in pain from her moans. We feel so helpless, how horrible to hear our mum in so much pain. When she finished she opened up the curtain and mum was sitting up but very sleepy.

The nurse tells us that mum is going to be moved shortly to the renal ward which is much better equipped for the dialysis and they can keep an eye on her kidneys, so we started getting her things together. The porter came about an hour later to move mum, they don't have to get her out of bed as they wheel her in the same bed which makes more sense. We went upstairs with mum walking behind her bed.

The Renal Ward is quite different to the orthopaedic ward, much brighter, more clinical looking and not dismal like the orthopaedic ward. Unfortunately, there are many ill people here and some have had kidney transplants, also the patients seem younger than in orthopaedic's. There are three other female patients in the ward who seem quite young, one has just had a kidney transplant who looks in her early 20's and two other ladies who look around 40ish. Mum will like that as she loves being with younger people and not anyone her own age.

Mum is seen by the registrar Dr Angus, a tall man who seems to be in his 30's. He tells us that mum's kidneys are working at just under ten percent which is due to painkillers, etc and they now have to get all the poisons out of her body otherwise the alternative (in his words) "It will be curtains for her" Excuse me, who the hell is this doctor, can you imagine how we feel? We never realised how very ill she was and what a way to tell us.

Mum was made comfortable and later she went on the dialysis machine which stays permanently next to her bed. It's a large white machine with lots of buttons, tubes and a monitor.

It will filter mum's blood to remove excess water and waste products. Blood is drawn through a specially created vein which is called an arterio-venous (AV) fistula. From the AV fistula, blood is taken to the dialysis machine through plastic tubing. The dialysis machine is like an artificial kidney doing the same work your kidneys do. Inside, it consists of more plastic tubing that carries the removed blood from mum to the dialyser, a bundle of hollow fibers that forms a semipermeable membrane for filtering out impurities. In the dialyser, blood is diffused with a saline solution which is in turn diffused with her blood. Once the filtration process is complete, the cleansed blood is returned to mum.

Mum was on dialysis today for two hours and seems to take it quite well. She is also talking to the other patients, which is a good sign.

Mums right arm

12th August: Mum went on dialysis again for two hours today but I am very concerned about her right arm.
A few years ago Mum fell and dislocated her right shoulder; it never really healed properly and now she only has limited use of her right arm. Because she has been in bed for so long her arm seems to be getting worse and she hardly has any use in it. If mum starts to slide down the bed she cannot now push herself back up with both arms. We try and make her comfortable every time we see her but its very worrying. What happens when we are not there? We have told the nursing staff to keep an eye on mum especially when she eats.

Angry

13th August: I phoned and spoke to the house doctor about 2pm today to see how mum was as I could not get hold of him before. Mum went on dialysis for two hours again today and he said she will be having physiotherapy soon to learn how to do her leg exercises in bed.
I went to see mum after work and boy was she irritable and very angry. She seems to be taking it out on me and using me as a verbal punch bag. I have to bite my tongue and not say anything but I can understand how she feels, it is so hard for her. She cannot get up not even to go to the toilet and has to use a bed pan. Incidentally, she sometimes tips it over in the bed and has to ring for the nurse to come and clean her and change her bedding. She cannot wash herself so she has to be washed by the nurses and unfortunately sometimes it's a male nurse. What's more, eating is now getting harder for her because of her arm and sometimes the food spills on to her nightdress, how degrading for poor mum. Mum has always been an able person and is

not happy at all that she is becoming so dependent. She seems to have aged years in the four weeks she has been in hospital.

X-Ray

14th August: My sisters and I visit mum tonight and she tells us an x-ray has been taken of her kidneys. She has been chatting to the other ladies in the ward today but clearly she is not happy.

Sore on leg

15th August: I spoke to the doctor in charge of mum today when I arrived and he said she had to go on dialysis for three hours as the x-ray showed her kidneys are still the same. The sore on her leg is not good and still has to be dressed which is painful. The physiotherapist wanted to get her up out of bed today but mum went down for a scan so unfortunately she missed them. My sister has brought her some food but she is not that hungry, we want her to eat while we are there as we can help her.

CHAPTER TWO

One Month in Hospital

16th August: 4 weeks in hospital, it seems so strange; we would never have thought that mum would still be here. I spoke Dr Kapur who said Mum's scan was good but the x-ray showed fluid on her chest; also the temporary port will have to be changed to a more permanent one for her dialysis.
Tonight mum is very irritable and angry again. She is not eating much and even the food we bring to the hospital she doesn't want. I have told her she must eat to keep up her strength but she is not interested. My sisters and I are finding it harder and harder to know what to talk about to mum, we don't want to talk about hospital stuff so it's just the general everyday things that happen.

Permanent Port

17th August: Mum had the new permanent port put in today and she was on dialysis for four hours. The time is getting longer and longer for dialysis now. The team that did Mum's hip operation came to see her tonight and they said they would arrange for her to have another x-ray on her hip to see how it is progressing. Mum is under two teams of doctors, the orthopaedic's and the renal departments. Sounds very confusing to me, I only hope that that are corresponding with each other.

Hammock

18th August: Mum said that she had been doing a few steps with the physiotherapist today and he told her she could go home next week. I am a bit confused as somehow I can't believe she was told that and according to the patient opposite, mum hasn't been walking today with the physiotherapist, she has only been sitting in the chair next to her bed. Is mum getting confused and disorientated? I will speak to the nurse.
When the nurses get mum out of bed they use an electric hammock lifter, it's a kind of sling that is put under Mum's bottom in bed which then hoists her up and over and down onto the chair. It's quite a performance and the nurses have to be available to do this.

Coming home?

19th August: It's Sunday and mum has told us that she's coming out of hospital on Tuesday and has asked my sister if she can bring her clothes and take her home. I asked the nurse and she said that no one has told mum she can come home so it's very worrying. We really don't know what to say when she asks "Where are my clothes?" We will have to make excuses such as "I forgot them" or "they are in the car, I will bring them up later". I don't think Mum realises that she can't even walk at the moment; if she was to stand up on her own she would fall over as the muscles in her legs are so weak. We cannot tell her that as we don't want to depress her even more so it's a bit of a game we are playing, how we hate to lie to her and how much longer can this go on for.

Fluid on lungs

20th August: I chatted to Mum on the phone from work today and she says she feels very unwell. Her hip has been hurting and she still has fluid on her lungs.

I rang Dr Mehra on the orthopaedic ward to tell him about mum's hip and how it was hurting her. He asked me to ring the registrar Mr Brown. I did and of course, he was unavailable so I left a message for him to ring me.

I telephoned the renal ward doctor to find out how mum's kidneys were doing and Dr Angus said her kidneys are now starting to work. Thank goodness, but she still has fluid on her lungs and he wants her to move around more as he is concerned that pneumonia could set in.

I eventually spoke to the registrar Mr Brown on the orthopaedic ward who said mum was supposed to have an x-ray today but didn't because of the dialysis. I protested that mum must have the x-ray on her hip as it could have dislocated again. The doctor said it's highly unlikely as she hasn't been moving. Oh really I replied, the last time mum's hip dislocated she had hardly moved.

She will be having the x-ray tomorrow morning.

Mobile phone

21st August: Thank goodness Mum has her mobile phone with her, it's our lifeline. At least my sisters and I can keep in touch while we're at work. Mum said she had the x-ray on her hip and also on her chest today. Apparently she has an infection on her chest now so she has been put on an antibiotic. Mum does suffer from hay fever and can get chesty, could that be why and I suppose lying in bed does not help. The results have not yet come back from her hip but she does sound stronger and has been out of bed sitting in the chair for a few hours.

When I went to see her in the evening she seemed to look a bit better, she had more of a colour on her face than the past few weeks and has been chatting to the other patients on the ward.

Moving back?

22ⁿᵈ August: Mum's hip results have come back and they are good, no dislocation, but she's still in pain. Dr Brown visited her and said mum needs to be back on the orthopaedic ward once her kidneys are better. Oh dear, she will have to move again but at least they will be able to work on her getting out of bed and start walking to build up the muscles in her legs.

24ᵗʰ August: No change

Bruises

29ᵗʰ August: Mum told me on the phone this afternoon that it was confirmed she will be transferred back to the orthopaedic ward today. She was put on dialysis for four hours again this afternoon so she may go tomorrow.
We arrived at the hospital tonight and after being with mum for about an hour a doctor came over wanting to take blood from her. He tried to put the catheter in her hand but the veins on the top of mum's hands are so very thin. It's difficult to take blood and as the catheter keeps on coming out its very painful for her. We noticed that mum's hands are covered in bruises. She was in so much pain as the doctor tried and tried to take the blood, eventually thank god the catheter stayed in. Poor mum, oh how she is suffering.

Losing one's dignity

30th August: When I arrived at the hospital tonight Mum was very distressed. She had slid down the bed and had been in the same position for hours because she couldn't push herself up. I asked why she did not call for the nurse and she replied she did not want to disturb them. I told her that is what they are here for to help you, so must not to be frightened to ask for help. But surly they would have seen how uncomfortable she was, just proves how often they check on her.

Mum also told me that she had a very bad tummy earlier in the day. She had asked the nurse for a bedpan but it didn't come and unfortunately she couldn't hold on much longer and messed in the bed. She said that the staff took over an hour to see her and clean her up. She was so embarrassed and felt degraded. How horrible to be in that situation.

The registrar Mr Brown from orthopaedics came to see Mum while I was there but mum seemed to think that she was in hospital for her knee. My mother did have a knee operation a couple of years ago and obviously she's getting confused. I told the doctor about Mum's bad tummy and how long it took the staff to see to her. It's terrible to lose all your dignity and find yourself lying in all that mess, this should never have happened. He was quite concerned and spoke to the sister on the ward. Also no one from physiotherapy came to see her today.

No appetite

1st September: As it's the weekend there is no physiotherapy today. When I arrived at the hospital I propped mum up and tried to make her as comfortable as I could. Her right arm is now getting very bad and she has very limited movement in it.

She also has no appetite and doesn't eat much. I brought her some food and some cake but she told us to put it on the side and would have it later. My sisters and I see mum at the weekend in shifts, so someone can be with her all day and up to late at night so she is not alone for that long. She also has visits from her grandchildren.

How germs spread

4th September: Mum is to be moved back to the orthopaedic ward as they think she will receive more physio there and they can keep a better eye on her hip. I arrived at the hospital at 6.30 in the evening and mum was still in the Renal Ward waiting to go down. I started to get all mum's things together from the cupboard near her bed; inside were her towel and nightdress. Unfortunately, she had a bad tummy again today and after being cleaned up the nurses threw her nightdress "which had been very badly soiled" back in the cupboard without putting it in a bag. How disgusting. Now I know how germs spread in hospitals. I always take Mum's washing home with me but I think I will have to throw her nightdress away and get her a new one. I told the staff nurse what I thought, I was very angry.

Dr Field came to see mum and said her kidneys were still not kicking in as they would have hoped so she may have to be on dialysis permanently. What a shock to hear that – and at her age! I am not sure that mum realises what Dr Field means as she really did not make much of a comment.

Finally the porter came to take mum down to the Orthopaedic Ward. She was wheeled in to a room on her own. I asked the nurse why this was and she said "When they transfer patients from one ward to another they keep the patients in isolation until they get the results from tests for MRSA and Clostridium Difficile". They should have thought about that when they threw her nightdress in the cupboard. I wonder why when mum first went in to the open ward in renal from orthopaedic's there was no isolation. Seems strange to me.

On her own

5th September: Oh dear, mum is getting confused again and thinks she is going home next week. She told me that a young doctor said she could go home. I spoke to the staff nurse just to be on the safe side and he said that no way would she be going home yet, but he did say they will be trying to get mum into a rehabilitation hospital not too far away from where we live. She will still have to be on dialysis three times a week and as the rehabilitation hospital would not have the facilities for dialysis mum would have to come back and forth to this hospital in an ambulance. She is still not walking and has to be hoisted out of the bed so I feel the travelling back and forth will be very hard for her.

Mum was very unhappy and stressed at being in a room on her own. She loves being with people and with no activity going on around her she seems to be deteriorating mentally and it's only been one day on her own.

My Birthday

6th September: It's my birthday today and what a horrible birthday it is. I always got a birthday card from my mother and we would spend it together. My ideal birthday present would be for mum to be well, walking and come home. When I went to see her I did not mention it was my birthday as she would have been so upset that she had forgotten; Being in hospital you lose all track of time, day, night, days, weeks, poor mum.

Moved back

9th September: At long last Mum was moved back into the open ward in orthopaedic's. She is now better in herself with other people and activity around her. She has been chatting to the lady opposite and they have been getting on very well. Even just watching the nurses doing their daily duties around the ward passes the time for her.

Water infection

10th September: Mum phoned me and said that she had seen a doctor and they think that she may have a water infection. I telephoned the staff nurse on the orthopaedic ward who told me it was the renal doctor that had noticed the infection and they were now waiting for the results.
The next few days there has been no change, hence me not writing anything.

CHAPTER THREE

Two Months in Hospital

13th September: I spoke to mum this morning and she was extremely confused which made me very concerned, she did not know where she was and some things she was saying I could not understand. I spoke to my boss Steven and asked him if I could take the afternoon off so I could arrange to go to the hospital to see the doctors. I am very lucky as he has been so helpful and said it was not a problem. I phoned the hospital and made an appointment to see Dr Field. Dr Field said mum has a water infection which would cause her confusion, she still has fluid on her lungs which could possibly be pneumonia and she has fluid on her ankles. Mum's blood pressure is very high too which is giving her a headache, but the good news is that her kidneys are starting to work unassisted. She still has fluid which has to come off but at least they are starting to kick in. Mum was put on antibiotics for the water infection and is given a water pill for the excess fluid. I also spoke to the orthopaedic doctor Dr Mehra and he said that Mum has a problem with a nerve in her leg as there has not been much movement.

Muscle wastage

14th September: I wanted to know more about what Dr Mehra had said regarding the nerve in mum's leg and phoned mum's orthopaedic consultant Mr Shah and left a message for him to phone me. He rang me back and told me that mum has bruising on two nerves in her leg and because she has been bedridden for so long she also has muscle wastage. Her legs need to get stronger but due to her kidney problems this has prolonged the healing process. Rehabilitation is a long way off at the moment; her kidneys will have to get better first.

Moved again

15th September: We are now being told that mum is being transferred back to the renal ward. When I asked why? A nurse said maybe they need the space which I find very bad. When mum got back to the renal ward she was this time put in a single room. I asked why she had been moved again and was told the renal doctor had requested it as they felt that even though her kidneys were a little better she still needed dialysis and it was better and easier for mum in this department. Well that does make sense.

Hysterical

16th September: Mum phoned me tonight, hysterical, unaware of where she was. She had been sleeping but woke up very confused, frightened and alone. She needed the toilet so straight away I telephoned the ward and spoke to a nurse who got someone in immediately. Mum phoned me back 15 minutes later to say they had brought in the bedpan but was she was still very upset and confused to know where she was. I tried to reassure her that she was in a hospital room right near the nursing staff.
All this moving back and forth from ward to ward is having a terrible effect on Mum mentally.

Summary so far

19th July: Admitted to the Orthopaedic ward.
11th August: Moved to the Renal Ward.
4th September: Moved back to the Orthopaedic Ward alone for five days which totally distressed her.
9th September: Moved to an open ward in Orthopaedics.
15th September: Moved yet again to the Renal Ward in a single room.

Distress

17th September: I spoke to another doctor Dr East on renal who had transferred mum back. He said that her kidneys were not doing as well as they had hoped for and if they have not improved within the next few days they will have to do a kidney biopsy. But I thought that her kidneys had been doing well.
I voiced my concerns about mum going from one ward to another and the distress it was causing her. He said that he was not aware of that. I also mentioned her condition regarding her physiotherapy care that she was not getting the physio regularly. I also pointed out that she was finding it hard to manoeuvre herself in bed due to her arm and this has to be looked into.

Clostridium Difficile

18th September: If I thought things couldn't get any worse they just have. My mother has just been diagnosed with Clostridium Difficile. We should have realised this when her tummy problems started about three weeks ago. The doctors say it's not severe and mum is being given the appropriate antibiotics. You read about this in the news papers, these germs that spread around the hospitals, how horrible but I really can see how this happens. Oh bring back the Hattie Jacques type of matron, hygiene is slacking in our hospitals in a major way at the cost of our own lives.

Not eating well

19th September: I phoned the nurse on mum's ward this morning and she told me that mum is being referred to a dietician as she is not eating well; she is also getting more and more depressed. My sisters and I are making sure that mum has one of us with her every evening and all day at weekends.
I am not sure what to do. Mum is under two departments, renal and orthopaedic. Her body and legs are so very weak we cannot even move mum to another hospital. Where would we move her to, no one would take her in with the tummy bug. We cannot move mum home as she has to be on dialysis regularly and would have to have live in care 24/7. We cannot afford to get private nursing and with all the equipment it would cost thousands upon thousands of pounds. Even if we could afford it that would not be an option as mum is too ill to be moved and with this tummy infection she is also in quarantine. She had a scan on her kidneys today so we will await the results.

Vicious circle

26th September: No change since the 19th and to be honest I have not felt like writing anything down it's so depressing seeing mum like this. The days are the same and her confusion worries me. She doesn't seem to remember why she is in hospital anymore. She is sleeping a lot and complaining that her neck is hurting her. She has to get stronger and while she still has the CD she cannot even have any physiotherapy, it's a vicious circle.

Clostridium Difficile gone?

29th September: No change since the 26th. I went to see mum and I also saw the renal doctor, Dr Field. She said they were hoping for some improvement in mums kidneys but there had been no sign of that. The scan has shown no improvement and by now they would have thought the kidneys would have improved. If this carries on Mum will have to be on dialysis three times a week for the rest of her life.
The Clostridium Difficile infection has now gone and they will soon be transferring mum back into an open ward, thank goodness. Soon they will also be looking into sending mum to a different hospital for rehabilitation and intense physiotherapy.

Must start writing again regularly

30th September: I have not been writing up my notes regularly. My goodness, now when I look back on my notes I realise how important it is to write everything down as it's so easy to forget.

So hard

1st October: We went to see mum tonight, she said she had a chest x-ray, don't know the results yet. We chatted about anything and everything, it's so hard to try and keep the conversation interesting.
2nd October: My sister went to see mum tonight and she said that she had an MRI scan today, so will find out more tomorrow.

Moved back to an open ward

4th October: Mum has now been put in an open ward with other patients. I spoke to the renal doctor who said that the MRI scan had shown that mum has slowing of the arteries, also it shows blocks of plaque in them which is normal in older people, but her condition has made this worse. Thank goodness her chest x-ray showed no signs of infection.

Sleeping

5th October: My sisters saw mum tonight, they said that she didn't look well and was sleeping most of the time.

Fever

6th October: It's Saturday and when my sisters and I went to see mum today we got a terrible shock, she looked very pale. Her eyes were closed and she was throwing the bed covers off and even though she looked like she was sleeping she was very agitated. She wanted to speak but couldn't open her mouth and she is so very weak she could hardly open her eyes. Dr Angus the registrar came to see her and took many blood tests. Oh, her poor hands, they just can't keep the needle in her veins, she also has diarrhoea again and her tummy is very tender. I only hope that the Clostridium Difficile infection hasn't come back.
Mum has a very high temperature and her blood pressure is very low. She definitely has got some kind of infection and we have to wait until all the tests come back to see which infection she has. She has been given another strong antibiotic in case it is Clostridium Difficile and

has also been given a different antibiotic in case it is an infection from the port which is inserted into her chest. Dr Angus said that apparently this is quite common so they cannot rule that out. Mum has also had an ECG which shows that her heart is beating very fast, I could have told them that. We left the hospital about 9 pm but I hated leaving her.

Blood pressure very low

7th October: We got to the hospital early as it was Sunday. No change in mum today, she still has a high temperature, her blood pressure is still very low and obviously she is very weak. She is not eating; her eyes are closed for the majority of the time and still has diarrhoea. The nurse gave Mum Panadol to bring her temperature down, which seems to have helped. She seems calmer than yesterday and not so aggravated but not in the mood to talk.

Confirmed, Clostridium Difficile is back

8th October: Now the doctor thinks that mum may have diverticulitis. Diverticulitis is small, bulging sacs or pouches of the inner lining of the intestine that become inflamed or infected. Most often, these pouches are in the large intestine which can cause bloating and cramps.
I wish they would make up their mind; it seems to me that they are pulling at straws. My sister is with mum this afternoon and she said she looks better than yesterday thank god. Mum is sitting up and speaking but is still very weak; she will be going on the dialysis machine soon.
 I have just got a phone call from my sister, it has been confirmed that

mum has Clostridium Difficile back again, to tell you the truth, I doubt if it ever went away. She is being moved back into an isolation room so my sister is getting mum's things together to move her yet again.

Male nurses

9th October: I rang the ward this morning to speak to the nurse to see how mum was in her new room. She said mum didn't have a good night; she had diarrhoea twice this morning and feels very ill. Her tummy is tender and she feels sick. When I went to see mum tonight she told me that she hates being cleaned by the male nurses, my goodness, so would I. She is also in a lot of pain from bed sores on her bottom.

Happy Birthday Mum

10th October: Today was Mum's 85th birthday. I wanted to make it as special as I could. Mum cannot have flowers in her room so I had the biggest and brightest balloons delivered to her room this morning to help try to make the day special. When my sisters and I arrived this evening mum put on a very brave face "bless her." It was so hard and we really tried to be happy and laugh. I played some music and started singing that sure was a laugh! And we had a birthday cake with nice bits to eat but mum did not want anything. She is still in pain as her tummy is still so tender and she's hardly eating a thing so she is very thin. This is the first time ever that our mother has looked her age. Oh, what a horrible birthday!

CHAPTER FOUR

<u>Three Months in Hospital</u>

11th October: I telephoned the hospital at 2pm and spoke to Mum's nurse June. She said she hadn't eaten any breakfast or lunch and had been sleeping most of the day. I told her Mum has to eat or she will just fade away, then I suggested she try to coax her to eat and help to feed her as she was finding it very hard to hold a fork because of her arm. The nurse also said that mum has not yet been washed and had told the nurses to go away. I told the nurse that Mum has to be washed especially with her having Clostridium Difficile. How I wish I wasn't working.
I telephoned again at 4 o'clock and spoke to mums nurse June again. Mum still didn't have anything to eat and the nurse told me the doctor had suggested that they insert a feeding tube, which goes up her nose into her stomach to get some nourishment down her; this is given to patients who cannot obtain nutrition by swallowing which is called a Nasogastric tube.
I arrived at the hospital after work at 6 and Mum had just woken up after sleeping on and off through the day. I tried to give her some food but she would only take a small amount. Then I spoke to the renal consultant Mr White who said that mum didn't have diverticulitis but had colitis due to the Clostridium Difficile. He also confirmed that her kidneys were not waking up and she would have to be on dialysis the rest of her life; he had written up for a feeding tube. Mum's nurse spoke to me and said that she had refused her medication this morning. When I asked mum about this she couldn't remember saying

no but her tablets were still next to her bed. She did not want to take them even from me but then I made out that they were her hay fever tablets.

The nurse came to insert the feeding tube but mum refused. I told her that if she doesn't want the feeding tube then she must eat to get better, but whatever I say it seems that she has had enough and is giving up.

Today also would of been my parents wedding anniversary.

Three Options

12th October: Mr White came to see mum tonight. He said that she had three options: One, she had the feeding tube, Two, eat what the hospital gives her or Three, eat the food that we bring in. If not, she will never leave the hospital and she will *die*. Talk about giving it to her straight! Mum just looked and stared.

I was asked to leave mum's room by the nurse while she cleaned and changed mum. I watched from the small window on the door. It was horrible, they have to move mum from side to side and it hurts her, especially when she leans on her bad arm. She was moaning in pain as they were moving her, she is in pain from her hip, her legs, her arm, and all I can do is stand and look, how could it have come to this. When I went back into the room mum looked clean and refreshed, she was sitting up and I gave her a cuddle.

Making an effort

13th October: Well what the doctor said yesterday seems to have worked; mum is now making an effort to eat. She has had breakfast and lunch and is making an effort with herself; she even wants me to file and paint her nails, so today I will give her a manicure. She said that she also wants to go to her hairdressers (she liked to go every week when she was home) and keeps on at us to make an appointment to take her there. We keep on making excuses as there is no way she can go. We are trying to arrange for mum to have her hair washed in her room. As it's a single room there is a bathroom on suite, not that mum has ever been in there. My sister used to be a hairdresser and has washed and set mums hair in the past but we need to clear it with the staff nurse first. We will need help from the nurses to get mum out of bed and over to the sink in a wheel chair. She has not been able to have her hair done so far since she has been in hospital as she has been too ill, but it's wrong to make her wait any longer.

A rash has appeared

14th October: When I went to see mum today she was very angry and was fed up being prodded about (well, if anything that's a good sign) and she was totally clear in her mind. But a rash has appeared on her body and it's making her itch badly. I have been scratching her back as she finds it hard to move her right arm; I wonder what this is all about?

Rash is spreading

15th October: Mum was on dialysis today but she feels very tired and is sleeping most of the day. The rash is now covering more of her body so the nurse said she will get the doctor to look at it.

All over mum's body

16th October: The rash has spread all over mum's body now, it's really irritating her and looks like large hives. The nurse has given her an antihistamine as the doctor said that it could be an allergy to one of the drugs she is taking. When we came to see mum the nurses where massaging cream all over mum's body from top to bottom, which seems to be helping slightly as her skin is also very dry.

Eyes red

17th October: The rash is really bad, it's now affected her eyes and making them very red and dry. The nurses are still massaging cream into mum's body but the antihistamine does not seem to be working. They will have to try and see what it is that is causing the allergy. Unfortunately it's going to be a bit of trial and error and stopping certain drugs and using others. We are scratching Mum's back and tummy which is relieving the irritation a bit but not much.

If all goes well

19th October: The nurse said that if all goes well tomorrow we can wash mum's hair and as its Saturday we will have more time in the day. We told mum about her hair and she was really happy. It's been so long since she has had her hair washed and felt human.
Mum's skin is still red but the rash seems to be getting better and going down. However, her eyes are still sore so the doctor has prescribed some eye drops.

Hair Washed

20th October: My sister and I arrived at the hospital about midday armed with a hairdryer, brushes, shampoo, rollers, just about everything to make mum beautiful again. We asked when it would be convenient for the nurses to help us as we needed the electric hammock to get mum out of bed and into the wheel chair; they said after lunch they could help us.

What a performance, poor mum. She has to lay flat on her back, and then turn onto her side so they can lay the hammock sling flat on the bed. Then mum is rolled back over onto her back. They then sit her up and belt her up to make sure it's secure. They then start the motor which lifts the hammock with mum sitting in it high above the bed which then moves around and then lowers mum onto the chair. Talk about a merry go round, it takes a good 10 minutes to get her out of bed safely.

We wheeled mum over to the bathroom and placed her head over to the sink so she was bending forward. It was very hard for mum to bend her head over the sink but she managed. Then with a shower attachment we washed her hair. Ohhhh, how lovely, my sister gave her a really good head massage. When she finished we wheeled mum back to her room and kept her sitting in the chair while my sister cut mums hair and rolled it up. We brought a portable hairdryer into the hospital which she put over mums head to dry her hair.

      Mum was always very particular at looking her best so this has made her feel so much better, a tonic in itself. When her hair was dry my sister combed it out and made it look really lovely. Mum felt so good when the nurses came in to say how lovely she looked, she was very happy, the happiest she has been in a long time.

I had a dream

21ˢᵗ October: The past months are starting to show on my sisters and I and I had the strangest dream in the early hours of the morning, so strange in fact that I had to jot it down on some paper next to my bed in the middle of the night.

Mum was standing on the pavement in the street and across the road was her doctor. Mum ran excitedly over the road to see him. I could not believe my eyes and ran up to Mum shouting "Mum, Mum, you can walk; you have just run over the road!" She looked down at her feet, smiled and said your right, I have. She was so happy.

When I next looked at her she looked really young (just how I remember when I was about eight years old). I put my hands on each side of her face and said, "It's so nice to have you back, we have all been so worried about you, and now we have you back again."

Mum phoned me this morning to tell me she had spilt all her breakfast down the front of her nightdress. Her arm is so bad she finds it very hard to feed herself. I phoned the nurse on the ward to go to see mum straight away and help her. Mum couldn't find her buzzer on the bed which alerts the nurses; thank goodness mum had her mobile phone next to her. I always make sure that her mobile is charged every day. That's the problem; as mum is on her own there is not a regular flow of nurses. How long would she have waited if she never had her phone to phone me?

Mum was sleeping when I arrived about 2 in the afternoon and woke up a couple of hours later. She was in much better spirits and eating more but her nose has been running a lot and we're not sure if it's a cold or hay fever as she suffers a lot from hay fever.

Ward closed due to outbreak

22nd October: Mum phoned me this morning at 7 o'clock complaining she felt unwell. She said she had a chesty cough.
My sister telephoned me at 4 and said she has just got to the hospital but they're not letting anyone in to visit as there has been an outbreak of diarrhoea. The hospital has cordoned off the renal ward to all visitors.
Oh great, now we cannot even see mum, what will she do? We bring her food, water, make sure she is comfortable, and keep her company. Without us she will be very depressed, oh what a worry it is.
I phoned the nurse to make sure that mum is looked in on regularly and to help her with her food and to make sure that mum is not sliding down the bed.

I've just telephoned Mum and she said she's sneezing, it sounds as if she has a cold. She told me that she is on dialysis at the moment and will be coming off soon. She is not happy that we cannot see her but she said she would rather that than catch something.

Sees no one all day

23rd October: My sisters and I went to see Mum tonight as we were hoping that we would be allowed to go into see her as she is in a room on her own but due to the outbreak of diarrhoea we were still not allowed to see her. I am so angry; she's in a single room and sees no one all day. I'm also worried about her chest as she still seems chesty. I gave the nurse Mum's clean washing and told her to give her our love.

Ward still quarantined

24th October: Mum phoned me very early this morning about 6 sounding very confused; she thought it was night time because it was still dark outside. Being in hospital for so long you get so institutionalised that every day is the same, night, morning and you have no recollection of time.

I phoned later to see if we could see mum but the nurse said that we couldn't as the whole renal department was still quarantined. I phoned Mum at 9am and she sounded better, not confused at all, but very upset that no one could come and visit her. She is having an x-ray on her chest today so let's hope she hasn't got a chest infection.

Going to see mum

26th October: Mum phoned me this morning and said she still has the rash on her body, it seems to have got bad again and it's been very itchy. She said she needs more bottled water and something nice to eat with a cup of tea. That was it; I was going to see my mother by hook or by crook. After work I left straight for the hospital with something for her to eat, drink and clean nightwear. I was determined to see her. The doors to the ward are always locked and you have to buzz the nurse's station for them to let you in, but when I got to the door outside the ward someone was just coming out luckily for me. I walked in and tried to dodge the nursing station but I was not that lucky. The nurse stopped me and said, "You can't come in here, we are still in isolation and high risk."

    I replied forcefully, I'm going to see my mother she needs me, you can't stop me! The nurse explained that I shouldn't go in but she could see that I meant business so she allowed me in providing I put on the plastic apron and gloves.

Oh, my God. When I got in the room I got the shock of my life. Mum looked like she had just come out of Belsen. Her face was white, the skin around her eyes was bright red and her skin was peeling off in chunks. She looked up in amazement, delighted and surprised to see me. I gave her such a hug and told her it was ok that I could see her. I gave her the food but she was too distressed to eat, she was worried that I would catch something. I tried not to show mum how shocked I was when I walked in and fought back the tears. Mum kept on saying you have to go so I did not stay for too long as I did not want to distress her even more but I made sure she was comfortable and that her phone was charged and the buzzer (which alerts the nurse) was next to her on the bed.

I saw the nurse on the way out and told her how shocked I was at seeing mum and I asked what is being done about mum's skin? She said that mum's skin may have flared up because of the dialysis and she may be allergic to the fluid solution that goes into the blood to clean it. The dermatologist was looking into it to see what treatment they could give her. She had also been given creams for her skin but they weren't working. They had been giving mum an injection before the dialysis to see if this would stop the allergy but that wasn't working.

The nurse also said they will soon be transferring mum back to the orthopaedic ward so she can have regular physiotherapy. *Oh no, they're not, they are not going to move my mother again.*

I asked the nurse, "Why can't a doctor phone me to keep me updated with Mum's condition?" She said that it's better if I phone them myself. Yes I do but I can never get anyone to speak to. I am always trying but they are never available, and who do I ask for?

There is no continuity, every two weeks the doctors change; they have a meeting to discuss the patients and then change over. The doctor on at the moment never saw mum before the rash appeared; he had not built up a relationship with her, he doesn't know about her mental state. For all I know he just thinks she is a senile old lady, he knows nothing about her character, nothing about MY MOTHER. How can they push mum from one ward to another? Don't they realise what it's doing to her mentally? Anyway, on Monday I'm going to phone the PAL department which stands for Patient Advice and Liaison Services. They are supposed to give you advice if you have a complaint within the hospital. Let's see if they can give me some answers from the head doctors of both the renal and orthopaedic wards: Enough is enough, I have stayed back for too long, but because mum's situation has been so awkward with her hip, her kidneys, the horrible CD infection it has been a vicious circle.

Should I have done more? At first I thought that the priority was for mum to be on dialysis when her kidneys were failing which unfortunately interrupted her physiotherapy which in turn hindered the healing process of strengthening her legs. Then she got CD which made her very ill and weak, too weak to get out of bed, which in turn again hindered the healing process of strengthening her legs. Now it seems that the muscle wastage in her legs is so bad, will she be ever able to walk again? Should I have done more, could I of done more?

A plucked chicken

27th October: I phoned Mum throughout the day and she seemed better in herself. She said that the nurses have massaged cream into her body from head to toe and added that she looked like a plucked chicken; her body looked all feathery from the skin that was peeling off. She said that she had some of the cake that I brought her with a cup of tea in the morning and had a nice lunch. She even enjoyed her supper so hopefully she is getting her appetite back.

When she was speaking to me I had to pinch myself, her voice sounded so strong and clear, the best she had sounded in months. It was as if she was back home talking to me, but then mum asked if we could go to M&S together to get her some clothes to wear today so she is still confused.

Her mind must slip in and out of reality. Mum knows that she is being looked after by nurses, but has times when she asks if we can go out to lunch, or if she can get a cab to the hairdresser's. Quite often when we are leaving she asks us to turn the light off in the kitchen and lock the door after us. I never say "But mum you're in hospital" I just cannot bring myself to do that, am I right? Your guess is as good as mine.

Before my mother came to this hospital she had all her faculties about her. She was an attractive smart 84-year-old lady who looked about 70 and was totally coherent. Now she looks like a 90-year-old, she has periods of memory lapse and confusion; she is extremely weak and thin and has lost a tremendous amount of weight. She is in constant pain from her legs; she is in pain from bed sores and weak from the Clostridium Difficile infection. She cannot walk and I doubt that she never will. She has completely lost the use of her right arm, and to add to all of this she will be on dialysis for the rest of her life.

My sister's dream

28th October:

My sister had the strangest dream; she dreamt that our mother was sill in hospital but in a wheelchair. She was sitting next to a filing cabinet which was next to her bed trying to find her medical notes. Someone was in mum's bed; it was our father wide awake, alive and well. (He passed away over ten years ago.)

PALS

29th October: I took the day off work today and telephoned the PALS department, unfortunately it was on answer phone so I left a message.

A man called John from the PALS department called me back and I explained my mother's situation. He suggested I put in an official complaint in writing and he also arranged for me to have a meeting that day with the renal ward doctor Dr Davies at 11.30. Unfortunately this was his last day as yet again he was handing over to another doctor Dr Harris as his two weeks were up.

I arrived at the hospital just before 11.30 and went in to see Dr Davies. I voiced my concerns about mum and said that I wanted a full update on mum's health. I also showed him a photo of my mother taken about a year ago. How lovely she looked, smart, glamorous; not like the lady that's now in that room. I wanted him to see how she has deteriorated it such a short time. I could see his eyes open wide when I showed him the photo of mum.

He said that mum's skin is now settling down, it seems that she was allergic to the ingredients in the dialysis fluid. They have now changed the ingredients which seem to be agreeing with her. He thinks the Clostridium Difficile has gone but mum has abnormal protein in her blood which they are looking into.

I told Dr Davies I didn't want mum transferred back to the orthopaedic ward as it was better for her to stay here in renal so she can have the dialysis in her bed without being moved, she has also got used to her surroundings and familiar with some of the regular nurses. The team from physiotherapy will have to come to mum.

When mum was last in the orthopaedic ward they had to take her to outpatients for dialysis. She hated that and was so very confused, it also left her open to infection. People that have just come in for day treatment are also with the in patients so I did not want mum getting a cold or anything else. I also said my mother needed to have regular physiotherapy and while I was there he arranged for me to have a meeting with the physiotherapist.

I saw the physiotherapist who said that they are trying to arrange mum's physio before she goes on the dialysis machine so she does not miss it.

Unfortunately, due to mum getting Clostridium Difficile, her skin reaction to the dialysis and the ward closing, mum's physio had been held up, but hopefully she will now start to get stronger and then they can work on her going for rehabilitation.

I tried to speak to mum's orthopaedic consultant Mr Shah who did the hip operation but he was away on leave for a week. I tried to speak to his registrar Mr Brown but he was in theatre. I had him paged later in the day but he didn't pick up so I will try again tomorrow. It's a case of out of sight out of mind for my mother's consultant and his team, well that's the way I can see it.

I then went into see Mum and stayed for about three hours. Even though the ward was still in quarantine they allowed me to stay. Mum was so pleased to see me, she was on dialysis at the time and looked much better; her skin was not red but still peeling. She was much brighter in herself but as the dialysis was finishing mum started to get confused again and she thought that she was at home. She was saying that she had to clean the kitchen and the lounge. I said don't worry I will do it. I was talking back to her as if she was at home as I didn't want to upset her. I told her the cleaning can be done later. I gave her back a good scratch on her back then the girls from physio came in to work on mum so I left. All in all quite a productive day I thought.

Steam cleaned

30th October: The wards have been steam cleaned to get rid of all infection and are open today for visitors. There's no call back from Mr Brown and I also left a message with his secretary to ask him to phone me. No one has yet phoned me back but John from the PAL department left me a message on my phone to say that another doctor, Mr Patel, was taking over from mum's orthopaedic consultant while he was away. I have tried all day to page him but he is not answering. I will speak to the PAL department tomorrow to see if they can get in touch with him.

Mum has had various x-rays of her bones today. She had been sleeping most of the day and when my sister came to see her she was still sleeping. Not only that but she has had no lunch or dinner. I rang the hospital at 10.00 pm to see how she was and she was still sleeping. They had checked her blood pressure and it was normal. I asked the night staff to keep a check on her throughout the night.

No more mobile

31st October: I went to Mum's home today to get her post as I do every week and noticed her mobile phone bill. She owes £60.00 which is a lot of money considering she hardly uses her mobile as we phone her the majority of the time. When I looked at the bill I could see that there were telephone numbers she had rung continually, just random numbers. I realised that mum cannot have her phone with her anymore; I can't take the chance of mum using the phone as she could end up phoning abroad and costing herself a fortune. I don't know what I am going to say to her.

I rang the nurse who is looking after mum today called Sam, it was a male nurse. He said mum hadn't eaten much breakfast this morning and they wanted to put a feeding tube into mum, but he was told my sisters and I had refused mum to have it. I asked him where he got this information from as we never had refused. I asked to speak to the staff nurse on the ward to find out about mum. She said she was not aware mum had not eaten yesterday. How bad is that? I said, why not, you should be aware of everything and it should be on her notes. I said can you please make sure that my mother has her lunch given to her and it's not just left on the tray, she also needs help when eating as she cannot move her right arm and that should also be on her notes.

I left a message for Dr Harris to call me, the doctor that took over from Dr Davies. He didn't ring me back, what a surprise. If my sisters and I did not have to work we would be at the hospital all day. We feel so helpless. I eventually got hold of him and I asked about the results from mum's x-rays. They had been taken because of the abnormal protein in her blood which could potentially affect her bones. Mum's right shoulder had shown that it's quite inflamed so they may inject her with steroids to help. The good news is that mum is much better on the dialysis since they changed the ingredients; they feel that it was the Heparin that mum reacted to so badly.

Call the police

1st November: Last night I had a terrible row with my sister; the strain of the past four and a half months is beginning to take its toll on all of us. She went to see mum last night and felt that the nursing staff were somehow distant to her. She felt they were getting fed up with all the phone calls I have been making to the hospital as I have been quite out spoken. She was also concerned that they would take it out on mum, oh come on, surely not! Whatever they may think of me they would never take it out on mum. How the hell can I stand back and say nothing? I reacted very strongly to her comments then decided to go to bed and sleep on it. I woke up still angry and determined not to just stand back and say nothing.

My son Darren said he phoned mum and she told him to phone me to say that I shouldn't come to the hospital tonight as she won't be there. I don't know what she means, maybe she is confused again, maybe she is going to another ward. Well I will find out when I see her later.

It's 6pm and I have just walked into mum's room. Oh my God! She's sitting slumped in the chair with her head on the bedside table. Her dinner is near her hair and all dried up. Mum's moaning and crying that she wants to go to the toilet and shouting "Call the police, call the police, get me out of here!" She's cold and her back is hurting her as she's so bent over.

      I ran out in tears shouting for the nurse to help then I ran back into mum's room. Mum was so distressed, she held on to me saying get me out of here. I put her dressing gown round her before comforting and cuddling her and rubbing her back.

The nurse came into mum's room and said she needed to hoist mum up with the hammock to get her back onto the bed but could only do that when one becomes available. I said how the hell could she be left like this. I kept on going outside mum's room to find out when the nurses would be coming in to see to mum. Half an hour later they came in to put mum back on the bed and clean her, disgusting.

 WHY, WHY, WHY IS THIS HAPPENING! SOMETHING HAS TO BE DONE. I had to hold back my tears as I didn't want to distress my mother further. Eventually mum calmed down. I helped the nurse wash her and we made her comfortable. I stayed for hours just stroking her face and cuddling her.

I took some photos with my mobile phone of the way mum was left in the chair slumped over otherwise no one would ever have believed me. God knows how long she had been left like that. I didn't sleep all night thinking about the way my mother was left for hours and the frightened look on her face. No way was I going to stand back and do nothing.

The letter

2nd November: I made a formal complaint to the hospital and sent it via email with attachments of the photos.

This is the state of the NHS today, the wards are understaffed and they have too many patients to look after. My mum is alone, the nurses forget to look in on her and leave her in that state? This is my mum. She is a human being but she has lost all dignity and is suffering badly. This should not be happening, there are no excuses. If a patient wants to go to the toilet and the nurses are with another patient they're left until it's too late.
My mother now has acute kidney failure; she has twice caught Clostridium Difficile and has been in Isolation three times. What's more she has had water infections, an allergy to the dialysis which caused her skin to erupt and will now have to be on dialysis for the rest of her life. She has completely lost her appetite which has led to a tremendous reduction in her weight. She is very weak and has bed sores and has not walked for four months. Her leg muscles are wasting away, and she has periods of confusion. All this because of the setbacks from the initial operation, which took place 20th July 2007.
Before my mother came to this hospital she had all her faculties about her. She was an attractive, smart, 85 year old woman with the mind of a 70 year old.

Points:

- 19th July 2007: Admitted to hospital.
- 20th July: Hip operation, X-ray was given soon after operation, results good.
- 23rd July: Physiotherapy starting but in constant pain, cannot walk.
- 2nd August: 2nd x-ray given.
- 3rd August: Results from x-ray show the hip has dislocated.

Examination shows that due to drugs (pain killers, etc.) my mother now has a problem with her kidneys. She needs more fluid for the kidneys to function correctly before a general anaesthetic for a second operation to have her hip manoeuvred back on 10th August.

- 4th August: Saline drip given. I spoke to Dr Murray and voiced my concerns
- 5th August: Too much fluid given resulting in breathlessness.
- 6th August: Drugs now given to relieve the excess fluid. Chest x-ray given.

A patient in ward said my mother was very confused, disorientated and breathless.

- 7th August: Given a saline drip.

The renal doctor visits my mother and finds her on a saline drip. She is furious that it had been administered and takes her off the drip straight away. Apparently the saline drip should have come off my mother's notes but it didn't.

My mother is still very breathless due to excess fluid. Now she is on an oxygen mask and told by the renal doctor that she may have to go on to a dialysis machine.

- 10th August: My mother went down to theatre to have her hip manoeuvred back. While under the anaesthetic my mother was given a port in her chest to be ready for dialysis.

Question

How could my mother's hip dislocate days after the operation? She could not even walk.
Why did she have to wait one and a half weeks for an x-ray when she was in so much pain after the operation?
If my mother had had an x-ray when she first complained of the pain she had in her hip, she would not have been given so many pain killers, which in turn have affected her kidneys.
Why was the saline drip still on my mother's medical notes to be administered when she was diagnosed that too much fluid had been administered?
My mother came to this hospital on 19th July. She has now been in here for four months and worse than when she came in.

Broke down

3rd November: I went to see Mum tonight. She had lost even more weight. She was very confused and appeared to have gone back in time and asked me if the boys were in bed. One is 26 and my other son is

22. I just said no as I realise that when she has these moments of confusion she is in her own little world and happy to be there, so it would be wrong of me to try and bring her out of it; it would just confuse her even more.
Mum is not eating and barely drinking. The hospital thinks that the dreaded Clostridium Difficile infection has come back again. They are waiting for tests to come back but she has had diarrhoea three times today so I am sure it never even went. I tried to make her eat and drink something but she just got very angry with me. Then she said, "Come on, let's go home, I'm tired and want to go to bed." She then tried to take her nightdress off and get out of bed. By now she was extremely confused and very restless.
I called the nurse to help me, a really lovely nurse called Sally. She remembered seeing Mum some months ago when she was sent down for dialysis from the orthopaedic ward. She was so shocked that mum was still in hospital and how much weight she had lost. Sally settled mum down and then she fell asleep. Sally sat down next to me and stayed for a short while. We chatted about Mum, how glamorous and attractive she was, and how we never would have thought that four months down the line she would still be in hospital in this condition. At that point I just broke down in tears; the past months had finally caught up with me. I suppose it was good that I let it all out; it's no good keeping your emotions bottled up inside you.
It was getting late and as I was leaving the hospital about 9ish mum appeared quite restless in her sleep. I really didn't want to leave so I chatted to the nurse who was looking after mum tonight and told her, "If you're concerned about my mother in the night please phone me, I don't care what time of night it is, just phone." And please check in on her often.

Nearly choked to death

4th November: It's Sunday and I got to the hospital about midday, Mum seemed calmer than yesterday. She was talking a bit but still very confused and not eating. At 4.30 my sisters and my son arrived, shortly after mum fell into what can best be described as a very disturbed sleep. She didn't relax until about 8 o'clock in the evening. At about 8.30 we went out of her room to speak to the nurse then went back to the room to get our things.
Thank goodness we went back because as we walked in to mum's room she was vomiting in her sleep. If we hadn't of been there she would have choked to death. I screamed for the nurse and she came running in. Mum looked so ill. She put mum on oxygen and gave her an injection for sickness. She then changed mum's nightdress and sheets. When she had settled and managed to go back to sleep we decided to go home. Mum definitely has the Clostridium Difficile back again.

Will not revive her

5th November: I phoned the hospital this morning and spoke to the nurse. She said that mum was not good and the doctors are very concerned about her.
When my sister arrived about 2 o'clock mum was sleeping but then woke up shortly afterwards and seemed to perk up. She asked if she could have a drink. Mum always used to like a tipple at night time. Oh my, does she make us laugh. My sister said, "Sorry mum, I don't have any with me." When the doctor came in to see her he was quite surprised to see mum sitting up. He took my sister outside and explained that Mum is very ill. He said they had decided that should she have a heart attack they wouldn't revive her as it could do her

more damage. They felt she didn't have much time left.

As much as a terrible shock it was to hear this our mother would never have wanted to live like this, I know she never would want to be revived. She cannot walk, she cannot move herself, she has to wear a nappy, she has lost all her dignity, she is in pain, she is on dialysis, she is losing her mind, and this will only be getting worse.

"Just let our mother go pass away peacefully, when she wakes up she will be in a wonderful place with our father and all her brothers and sisters waiting for her, she can then dance once again, be beautiful and happy"

I left work at 5.30 and arrived at the hospital to find mum sleeping but in a disturbed way again. The nurse has now asked us all to wear a disposable plastic apron and surgical gloves when we enter mum's room to stop the spread of infection which are kept outside the room. We always use the antiseptic hand gel when we arrive and when we leave the hospital which is in a dispenser on the walls of the hospital, but it sure is not working.

The nurse said that mum had refused dinner before I arrived. My sons and my other sister came and mum woke up for a short time. She opened her eyes, looked really surprised at us and said, "What are you all doing here" She then put her head back and went back to sleep. We left about 8 o'clock as she appeared to be sleeping peacefully now.

Feeling guilty

6th November: My sister went to see mum this afternoon and found her quite alert; she had a few bits to eat but then complained of indigestion. I arrived with my other sister about 6 o'clock after work as mum was just coming off of dialysis.

We were all talking about anything and everything but mum was still a bit confused and going back and forth in time. When we were about to

leave mum said, "Well come on, let's go, we can't stay here all night."
It was quite funny actually, we all looked at each other sat down and
said we're not going yet.
Mum replied, why, I want to go home.
I know you do mum I said, but let's stay here for a while.
I called the nurse to come in and she took mum's blood pressure. She
found it was very low and said that she would keep a check on it. We
waited until we knew mum was comfortable and falling asleep, we
then left.
We feel so guilty when we leave mum but obviously we have to, I
would stay all night if I could.
I forgot to have lunch today, that's no good. When I got home I had a
plateful of pasta then fell into bed. I must look after myself as I have
lost nearly a stone in weight and I can't afford to collapse. Tomorrow I
will make sure I eat lunch.

The reply

7th November: Just received a reply to my formal complaint from the Hospital. It reads as follows:

Dear Ms Slater,

Thank you for your letter dated 2nd November in which you raise concerns regarding your mother's care at our hospital. The matters you have raised will be investigated through the NHS complaints procedure by Mrs Adams, Operations Manager, Surgery Directorate of the Trust.

In accordance with the Trust's policy for dealing with formal complaints we aim to respond by 10th December 2007. If we are unable to provide a complete response by the date specified, we will write to you again explaining the reasons for the delay.

However, as we are anxious to maintain patient confidentiality, we will need signed consent from your mother that you have permission to discuss matters relating to her care. In the meantime, we will continue with our investigations but no details will be disclosed until written consent is received.
For your information, I enclose a leaflet, which outlines the NHS complaints procedure operating within the Trust.
Yours sincerely

Mary Darlington
Patient Affairs Co-ordinator

I paid particular attention to paragraph 3:

"However, as we are anxious to maintain patient confidentiality, we will need signed consent from your mother that you have permission to discuss matters relating to her care"

Are they mad, what do they want me to do? Ask my very ill, weak and confused mother (who I might add, no longer realises she is in hospital) to sign a form reminding her of the four months she has already been in hospital. From the time she had her hip operated on then her kidney failure, then contracting Clostridium Difficile. She could not even hold a pen and write. Why would I have to completely stress her out by taking her out of the world she has gone into and back to reality. I DON'T THINK SO.
I did send back the signed consent "signed" – but it wasn't my mother that signed it.

Chapter Five

Four months in hospital

It's party time

8th November: When my sisters and I went together to see mum last night we found she was a bit down. She was asking the nurse for a little whisky (to touch the heart shall we say)
My sister went out to see the nurse and asked if she could have one, after all if it makes her happy. The nurse said if it was up to her she would give mum anything she wanted.
Well that did it; my sister went out to M&S and came back with party Nuts, crisps, olives, you name it and a little drop of something. Mum was so funny, you should have seen her face when we took everything out of the bag, it was the old mum back again. We all had such a giggle, it was lovely and it was the best we have seen her in months. Like they say, 'A little bit of what you fancy does you good' and it sure did. Then mum surprised us all, she said "Who would have thought it, me of all people to be a cripple?" God knows what goes on in mums mind when she is all alone in her hospital bed.

Quality of life "Zero"

9th November: I phoned the hospital this morning. Mum didn't sleep until about 3am, maybe it was all the excitement, but I was told she's

much brighter this morning compared to yesterday.
Apparently the doctors have been talking about putting a tube up Mum's nose to get some food down her. Mum says she doesn't want this done. The nursing staff have tried but she is getting too stressed. I'm trying to get hold of Dr Harris today to voice my concerns. Yet again we have communication problems and I left a message with his secretary.

Dr Harris did return my call; wow! He said that if mum does not have any nutrition she will always be in hospital (in other words she will die here). I said that my sisters and I do not want her to suffer any more; a tube put up her nose would cause her too much stress. He suggested a tube in her tummy or neck.

Effectively, Mum now only has one limb on her body she can use, her left arm. Her legs are twisted from being bedridden for so long and she has no use in her right arm and shoulder. She is very weak as a result of the Clostridium Difficile and has terrible bed sores on her bottom; she also has a bad sore on the heel of her right foot. The daily routine of washing her is painful, she suffers every day when she is moved from side to side when being given a bed bath. Mum is still in isolation because of contracting Clostridium difficile. As there's no life going on around her, mums memory is starting to lapse in a major way. Her quality of life is zero.

I said to Dr Harris, "Please don't carry out any other procedure on mum until you have spoken to me and my sisters." I also commented that I knew his two weeks on the ward should soon be up. Dr Harris acknowledged this and replied by saying he would be handing over to Dr Williams on Tuesday. I asked him to relay all my comments to him. When we went to see Mum tonight we found her looking very tired. She was still on dialysis and was quite confused. I was sitting next to her on the bed, stroking her face. We left about 8pm after she had gone to sleep.

Better spirits

10th November: Mum was in much better spirits today. Her colour was better but she had not eaten much. We brought her a nice smoked salmon sandwich which she enjoyed, some fish balls but she didn't want the soup my sister had made. She seems to be happier eating small bits and not a main meal. She was much more alert but still seemed confused.

Fingers stiff

11th November: Mum is quite good again today, hardly eating but she did enjoy a half smoked salmon sandwich again. She is talking about "years ago" as if it is the present so we just keep the conversation going the way she can relate to it. Her hand and shoulder is really hurting and her fingers are getting stiff. I must speak to the doctor to see if they can do anything to ease the pain.

Slid down the bed

12th November: Mum has been on dialysis today. When I went to see her this evening she was very cold and uncomfortable having slid down the bed, I really don't know how long she had been like that. I

keep on telling the nurses to look in on mum regularly but do they? I moved mum up and wrapped her up with more covers and tried to make her as comfortable as I could. The nurse had a word with my sister today and said that Dr Angus had spoken to Mum and asked her if she would have the tube put up her nose. Apparently mum had said yes. We were very surprised to hear that and obviously as mum is still very confused I just wanted to know if she realised what had been asked of her. I asked her if she remembered what the doctor had said and I wasn't too surprised when she said she wasn't sure. But then she remembered and said, "No, I don't want it, I am so tired."
"I know you are, mum," I replied and you don't have to have it if you don't want it, but you have to eat. Oh, how I could have cried.

Guinness

13th November: I rang to speak with Dr Angus and arranged to have a meeting with him and my sisters for the following morning at eleven o' clock.
Mum is looking good tonight. She had some lunch earlier and we gave her a Guinness (on nurse's orders). Oh boy, did she lap it up! She also had a large piece of bread and some thick vegetable soup. She was happy and comfortable and eventually went into what seemed to be a nice peaceful sleep. I put the Guinness in the hospital fridge and asked the nurses to give it to her along with her lunch tomorrow.

No to the feeding tube

14th November: - We had the meeting with Dr Angus today. At first he said he would only talk to us seated around mum's bed, why I don't know. I explained we had a few issues to address and we needed to sit down with him before we went into see mum. He really didn't want to do that but I was quite forceful. We explained that we only want what's best for our mum and we didn't want her to be under any more stress, we didn't want the tube to be inserted into her, mum doesn't want it; even when she says yes she then says no and she is also starting to eat more and enjoying what we are bringing in for her so it's not an option. He explained that without food mum will get pneumonia but agreed not to have the tube forcefully inserted as long as she is eating.
We also spoke about her arm, as it is quite painful, and the Clostridium Difficile which she still has. I said we didn't want her moved again. He confirmed that she would not be moving to another ward and she would stay in the renal ward in her own room which has now become very familiar to her.

No more prodding

15th November: Since we have been giving mum what she fancies she is now getting back a little appetite and is eating some of the food we bring in. No more prodding, no more poking, no more stress, let's just allow her to be happy. She is asking about my dog Max, oh how I would love to bring him in to see her but I know I can't. I know it seems silly but even my dog is missing the Saturdays at nannies, am I sad or what!

Leave me alone

16th November: Mum was on dialysis again when my sister arrived today but she didn't want anything to eat. When I got to the hospital tonight mum was quite confused, but she did have some of the soup eventually.

The nurse came in to wash mum but she wasn't happy and said, "Leave me alone, I'm fed up of being pushed and shoved!" Oh dear, and I said no more prodding. We calmed her down and then I helped the nurse wash her. I'm sure mum knew how very ill she was. We made mum comfortable and she went to sleep with me cuddling her laying half on the bed and I nearly fell asleep myself. My goodness, it reminded me of when my boys were babies and I had to lie on the bed with them to get them off to sleep. She had a lovely smile on her face and I stayed for quite some time.

I love my mother so much; it's terrible to see her suffer like this. My sisters and I have made sure that mum has one of us with her every day but we can't be with her 24/7, we have to work and the strain is showing on all of us, we feel so helpless.

Strong Lady

17th November: It's Saturday and my sister phoned me this afternoon to say that mum seems much better today. It's like a rollercoaster, one day good, one day bad. I didn't go to the hospital today as I was shattered; one of my sisters went this afternoon and one was going this evening. Mum's certainly a strong lady and seems to be pulling through. I went to bed this afternoon and boy, did I need it. My cousin Joceyne came over this evening and after we had shared a bottle of wine and a takeaway Chinese meal together, I finally returned to the land of the living.

I feel better

18th November: I feel a lot better today, it's amazing what just one days rest can do. How terrible thinking of myself with poor mum in hospital. We all got to the hospital about 2ish and stayed till quite late. Mum had her Guinness with a nice big lump of cheese, it looked so good to eat that I joined her.

Am I going bonkers?

19th November: Mum's the same, holding her own, thank God. I thought it was about time I gave the Centre an update on my mother. I work there voluntary once a week on a Monday night for a few hours giving support to people who have health and stress problems. I haven't worked for over four months now since my mother became ill and I miss them all terribly.

Here's the email I sent.

Hi,
I thought I should let you know what's happening with me at the moment. My mum is quite an incredible lady. Two weeks ago the doctors thought she did not have long to live. She pulled through, bless her, but she is no way out of the woods.

She is hardly eating and she still has the hospital infection Clostridium Difficile.
She is on dialysis 3 times a week and only has the use of one limb, her left arm.
She is very weak and if she gets any other infection her body will not be able to fight it.
She is now in her own little world but even though she is very confused as to where she is and why, she comes in and out of reality, but thank goodness she still knows all of us.
Bless her, on Saturday she thought she was at my house and when I told her where she was she said, "Am I going bonkers?" She then asked why was she in hospital. I said it was her kidneys as she still doesn't know that she has lost the use of her legs.
It breaks my heart every time I leave her at the hospital. On Friday she was very tired and wanted to sleep. I said, "Come on, let's have a sleep together and put my head close to hers. She asked me to sleep with her that night so I said, "Yes, Mum, let's sleep together" and I cuddled her.
Then she said, "You must be exhausted." I replied, "I'm okay."
She said to me, "You're beautiful" and asked to hold my hand. I gave her my hand and she took it to her lips and kissed me. She asked, "Will you sleep at my house tonight?"
She thought she was home so I said, "Yes Mum." I cuddled her until she fell fast asleep.
I miss you all but at the moment I cannot come back, I do hope you understand.
Jo x

The same

20th - 21st November: No change with mum and not much to report, but she does seem like she has a cold coming on; we will have to keep an eye on that.

Confused

22ⁿᵈ November: Tonight Mum seems more confused than ever, she said that the doctor spoke to her about going to a home. She also said that she has been waving at the man in the next block who she sees outside the window. There is no one there but mum seems to think there is. Anyway I will let her believe it, what harm can it do.

I had another dream.

23ʳᵈ November: *I was at the hospital with Mum, she was in bed as usual and asking to get out of bed. I told her she would have to wait; she then put her legs over to the side of the bed and stood up. I couldn't believe my eyes. Mum's legs are so weak but she could stand. She then took a few steps and started walking. I was so excited and called the nurse – then I woke up.*
Not much to report on mum today but I will phone the doctor tomorrow and tell him about mum and her state of mind.

Stay on dialysis or not!

24ᵗʰ November: I rang and spoke to Dr Angus. He said he had not told mum she could go home and that it was not an option now. He asked if I'd received a phone call from the clerk to see if we could have another meeting with him to review mum's situation. I never did get that call; still, I was on the phone to him now. He said they had to decide whether mum stays on dialysis or not. I knew that one day it would come to this, so with that in mind my sisters and I are going to have a meeting with him on Monday 26th November at 11.00.

Wanting to go out for lunch

25th November: It's Sunday and Mum is very angry today, she wanted to get up out of bed and go out for lunch. I told her that she couldn't go as she was in hospital. She said, "I will do what I want to do, if I want to go out for lunch I will go, if I want to go on holiday I will go. She was very agitated and was trying to get out of bed but could not move as she has no use in her legs so she was throwing the bed covers off with her good hand. We tried to calm her down which took quite a long time but eventually she settled down.
It seems that mum really does know what's going on and part of her is admitting it. She seems to be fighting within herself which is making her very confused.
Mum had some soup and later on I stroked and massaged her head, I also rubbed cream into her arms and legs as her skin is very dry. She really enjoys that and when I was leaving my other sister took over.

Just sock it to her

26th November: We had the meeting with Dr Angus this morning. He said that he asked mum if she would like to go on dialysis today, and she replied, "If it is good for me I will." He asked us about our feelings and how we felt about mum still having dialysis?

I said, "While she is still comfortable and not in pain we only want what's good for her."

Mum is not senile, she knows who we all are but she's very confused. If she starts to really deteriorate we will have to review the situation. We also stressed that she cannot be moved to a nursing home as that was her greatest fear. Ever since we were young she always said, "Never put me in a home." Dr Angus said they would not move her; to pass away unhappily would not be an option. As long as she stays in the hospital, at least she will be comfortable in what are now familiar surroundings. We will speak again at the end of the week.

My sister went to see mum this afternoon. She said mum seemed quite down; apparently she was not on dialysis today and had slept quite a lot. She told my sister that this morning the doctor had told her she had been very ill and if she is not on dialysis she will die.

My sister went to see Dr Angus and asked him what he had said. He told her he had said: "YOU KNOW YOU HAVE BEEN VERY ILL AND YOU WILL HAVE TO BE ON DIALYSIS FOR THE REST OF YOUR LIFE OR YOU WILL DIE; AND IF YOU DON'T EAT YOU WILL DIE, AND YOU CAN CHOOSE IF YOU WHAT TO BE ON DIALYSIS OR NOT."

What does he think he's doing? He didn't tell us he was going to say that to our mother, how dare he say that, why did he say that? It has put mum into a complete depression. He said "Well that's what we do now; it gives people time to say their goodbyes."

You hear time and time again that doctors speak to the patients and tell them all the facts without knowing how the patient will take that kind of information. Just sock it to them without giving a thought to how they will take it. PATIENT'S RIGHTS? HOLD ON A MINUTE, I THINK NOW THEY HAVE GONE TOO FAR. My sister went back to mum and tried to reassure her, but she just wanted to sleep. I arrived with my son's Darren and Paul tonight, and when mum saw them she gave them a wonderful smile which lifted her spirits and she then had some soup.

I will pop off soon

27th **November:** When I went to see mum tonight, she was lovely and very talkative. We had a drink together and then she had some soup, she seems to take that better than solid food with a nice piece of bread dipped in. She said, "You know with all my illnesses I will pop off soon but I will always be with you." I couldn't believe my ears, what did she say? After what Dr Angus had said to her yesterday she must have been doing a lot of thinking. I went to the bathroom and cried my eyes out. I then pulled myself together and went back inside and sat down on mum's bed and gave her a cuddle.
We had the most wonderful conversation so far and I think she was ready for it. Like me she is quite spiritual even though mum always said she was not sure if she believed there was a life after death, but in her heart I know she did believe, she was just frightened of it.

I told mum we all have to go sometime but when we pass we will be going to a most wonderful place. There are beautiful flowers with wonderful colours and everyone is very peaceful. We are not in pain anymore and can run and dance as much as we want. I told mum that she will see Daddy, Grandma, Grandpa, all her brothers, sisters and everyone she knew. Hey, they can have a party up there.
Mum said, "We must have a code when I'm gone so you know I'm around. Okay I replied, but we don't really need a code mum as I know you will always be with me.
But mum was adamant that we had a code so I told her what code we

could have and she agreed. I chatted with her how this life is a school and how we are brought here to learn. Someone who had been born into this life and never experienced any illness or hardship would never learn about life and have compassion for others. When we die, we go home (back to spirit). Mum said that no one ever comes back to tell us how wonderful it is. I said, "Can you imagine mum if they all came back to tell us how wonderful it is? Everyone would say, 'I'm not staying here on this earth anymore, I'm going up there because it's a much better place. Can you imagine, everyone would want to pop off and go. Well did she laugh! We spoke about loved ones that had passed over but we would be seeing them again and she was really happy.

When I left, mum went into the most wonderful peaceful sleep; she was smiling so beautifully I even took a photo of her with my mobile phone.

Mum Told her legs don't work

28th November: Why is it that the doctors decide what they say to their patients without consulting the next of kin? Mum has been feeling very depressed as she has been told by the doctor's that her legs don't work. How must she be feeling? Confused, lost, frightened, this is no way for anyone to suffer.

She has been sitting out of bed all day. The nurses had the hammock to hoist her out of bed and they will put her back to bed after supper.

New Doc on the Block

29th November: A new doctor has been assigned to the renal ward, Dr Smith. I have tried to contact her but so far I have not been able to speak to her. I will try again tomorrow.

Will have to move mum

30th November: I rang Dr Smith and was able to speak to her. She seems quite a hard and inaccessible person with no bedside manner. Her voice has no softness to it and she sounded very stern. She said my mother cannot be in hospital indefinitely and as she is starting to eat they will have to start making plans to move her. I mentioned that Dr Angus had said she could stay in her room in the renal department, and repeated what he had said to me, namely, there are two types of death; a good one and a bad one. So as we told him that mum would not last a day if she was moved he said she would be able to stay in her room in the renal department. I was so very angry and said to Dr Smith that I didn't want our mother to be moved. The conversation went round in circles and I could see that this doctor was adamant that mum should be moved.
The hospital got her in this mess, it's the hospitals responsibility to look after her, mum would not last two minutes having to be moved for regular dialysis and the discomfort alone would be cruel and she would suffer badly.
I went to see mum after work and when I arrived I asked if Dr Smith was still on duty. Let's see this doctor face to face I thought. She was still on duty, so I took the opportunity to speak to her. I asked the nurse where Dr Smith was and went up to her and introduced myself. She looked how she sounded; I really did not like this woman. Once again I explained my thoughts but still she said that mum would

eventually have to be moved to a home. I asked her what she thought mum's life expectancy would be and she replied "I'm not God, but people can live up to 30 years on dialysis".

For goodness sake, my mother is 85 years old, even if she wasn't on dialysis she wouldn't live another 30 years – can you believe that! Here is an intelligent woman talking a load of crap, I needed time to think, I needed time to stall her. Then I said, "Before my mother started to deteriorate, she was going to go for rehabilitation in a hospital near to where I live. She said maybe then that could be an intermediary stage. At least now I had time on my side. I then went in to see Mum and she was very confused again.

Letter regarding my formal complaint

1st December: I received a letter from the Hospital regarding my formal complaint:

29th November 2007

Dear Mrs Slater,

I write further to your letter of 2nd November 2007 in which you raised concerns regarding the care of your mother.

The investigation into your concerns is currently underway; however, as your mother remains an in-patient here, the investigation manager has been unable to access her medical records, which are required to assist with the investigation.

I would therefore be very grateful if you could grant an extension of two weeks beyond the date I originally specified (10th December 2007) so that we can fully investigate all your concerns and respond to you appropriately.

You can write to me at the above address or email me. If I do not hear from you I will assume that you agree to this extension.

*Yours sincerely
Mary Darlington*

It's Saturday and I arrived at the hospital about 2.45. Mum was sleeping and looked terrible. I kissed her forehead and stroked her head gently to try to wake her up. She looked at me, said a few words which I couldn't understand then went back to sleep. She woke up about 5 o'clock and said her neck was hurting. She had been sleeping in a funny position so that must have made her neck ache. She had not eaten any breakfast or lunch and not yet been washed. I asked the nurses to come in and wash her and when she was comfortable I got her a cup of tea. She also had a nice cream cake I brought her, but she really did look terrible; her skin was grey and she had aged even more. Later I gave mum some dinner but she was not happy and did not want to talk. She was very depressed and fell back to sleep about 7 pm.

Dad's Birthday

2nd December: Mum is still the same, very sleepy and not wanting to talk much. It would have been our late father's birthday today. How would he have felt seeing mum like this?

Vomited

3rd December: Mum seemed better tonight when I got to the hospital. The nurse said that she had been on dialysis again for four hours. I gave mum some soup, but she said she felt like she was going to be sick and then with that she vomited. I screamed for the nurse, "Nurse Nurse please help" they came in straight away and saw to mum. They cleaned and put a new nightdress on mum and clean bedding on the bed, but what a performance cleaning her and changing the bed. They made me stand outside; it's so horrible to watch. When they allowed me back in the room mum looked better but said that her leg and everything else was hurting her. She still has an open sore on the heel of her foot which has been there for months, the result of being in bed for so long and it's really painful. I calmed mum down, gave her a cuddle and was stroking her face until she then drifted off to sleep.

My reply to the hospital (sent by email)

4th December

4th December 2007

Thank you for your letter of 29th November 2007

Surely, if my mother is in the hospital, so are her medical records which must make it easier to access, also am I led to understand that all medical records are now computerised!

My concern is that my mother was given too many painkillers and put on a saline drip unnecessarily causing acute kidney failure and now having to be on dialysis three times per week, without which she would drift into a coma. I was equally concerned when I made my original complaint: 'Why did it take so long for my mother to have an x-ray to diagnose the dislocation of the hip?' and 'How could her hip have dislocated so soon after the operation?' The only form of movement she had was when the physiotherapist came to see to her after the first operation. My mother is very ill, she is in constant pain with bed sores, and she has lost the use of her legs completely. The fact that my mother has been moved so many times, I would not want her to be moved away from the Renal Ward as this in the past has added to her confusion and deterioration.

When my mother was moved back to the orthopaedic ward and had to be wheeled in her bed to the dialysis unit, this made her extremely distressed and open to infection. If she was moved away she would have to suffer the stress of coming back and forth in an ambulance 3 times a week to your hospital for dialysis, and as she is now so incapacitated and confused she would be very frightened and would not last long.

I await your reply

Joanna Slater

The hospital email reply

Dear Mrs Slater

Thank you for your e-mail. I have passed on your comments to the investigating manager.

At present, medical records are not yet computerised and must remain on the ward the patient is on. It is therefore difficult to retrieve them for a significant amount of time to enable relevant staff to review them and respond to the complaint.

However, we will aim to respond to you as soon as possible and I would like to apologise for the delay.

If you have any queries in the meantime, please do not hesitate to contact me.

Kind regards
Mary Darlington

Wanted to sleep

5th December: My sister went to see Mum last night; she was sleeping and did not want to be woken up. When she did wake up my sister tried to give her some soup, but she didn't really want anything and went back to sleep. When my sister left she saw the staff nurse, and was very upset. She said, "What's it all for, to give her another bit of mashed potato?"

When we last had our meeting with Dr Angus I asked him, "Would you still give your mother dialysis if she was in this condition? And his answer was no. Mum has no quality of life left, I wish she would now just go to sleep and not wake up. Oh mum, how did this all happen?

We all went to see Mum tonight, she was awake but very confused and she had been on dialysis for four hours again.

Chapter Six

Five Months in Hospital

In her own little world

6th December: I should have gone to see Mum tonight but I am aching from top to toe. I think I have some kind of gastric flu so no way can I see mum like this, but sisters are still going. One of them phoned to see how mum was this afternoon. The Matron of the renal ward picked up the phone. She had spoken to my other sister the previous week and was very kind. She said that if we have any concerns or issues we could speak to her. She would be away on leave from tomorrow till 17th December. It's really strange but I don't remember ever seeing her before.

I telephoned the Matron and told her that Dr Smith was talking about moving our mother and added that this was out of the question. She said she would ring me when she came back on December 17th and arrange to see my sisters and me.

My sisters told me that mum was very happy tonight but now totally in her own little world.

No Change

7th December: No change in mum, not much to report. I still am not feeling well so will not go to the hospital tonight.

Hello Harry

8th December: Mums brother Harry and sister-in-law Betty came to see her today, they come quite often in the day and mum is happy to see them.
She seems quite together but not really eating and is still in a lot of pain especially when the nurses have to wash her. Mum's niece Helen also came with her husband Gerry but are so upset to see mum this way.

Left hand hurting

9th December: I phoned the hospital and the nurse said Dr Smith wants to speak to me and my sisters, I think it's about making plans to move her, no way do we want Mum moved.
We went to see Mum, and her good hand is now hurting her, it looks as if it could be rheumatics.

Die with dignity

10th December: Dr Smith rang me about 2 o'clock at work today. I was really ready for an argument with her so I took the phone call in my boss Steven's office, but no way was I prepared for what she was about to tell me. She said that Mum had not made any progress and was still very confused. Mum didn't know when she was on dialysis and was therefore unable to make a decision as to whether or not she should still be on it.
    Dr Smith was hoping that since she came onto the ward nearly two weeks previously mum would have improved but she had

deteriorated mentally. She cannot see that being on dialysis is doing her any good. All it is doing is prolonging her life and adding to her suffering. She feels that our mother should die with dignity. If the truth be known my sisters and I also feel this, but it's still our mum, our mum who we love. It doesn't matter how prepared you think you are, it still comes as a terrible shock when you hear it from the horse's mouth (so to speak).

Dr Smith told me, "If mum stops the dialysis, she will slip into a coma sometime between 8 and 40 days then pass away peacefully." She will be monitored regularly and will not suffer. I told her that I had to speak to both my sisters and I would speak to her tonight when we arrive at the hospital. I phoned both my sisters and told them what Dr Smith had said and obviously they were very upset, but we all agreed, this has to be a joint decision, this is what mum would have wanted. Believe me; if our mother was standing in the corner of her room looking at herself she would be horrified, she would never want to carry on like that. She would say "for goodness sake, don't let me suffer like this anymore". I feel sick that it has now come to this.

We all went to see Mum tonight. My son was there when we arrived. They had put Mum on dialysis and she looked lovely. She seemed somehow to know what decision we had made without saying anything.

We went to see Dr Smith and told her our joint decision that we felt it best that the dialysis should stop as long as our mother would not suffer.

It was so hard knowing what to talk about sitting round mums bed, so hard not to show the upset on our faces.

      When we got up to leave, mum started getting stressed again. She wanted to get out of the bed and come with us; it was just heartbreaking. *Is this the right decision we are all agreeing to?* I thought. *What is the alternative?* If mum were to stay on dialysis, what quality of life would she have? She can't walk, she can't feed herself, she is in constant pain, she is confused and losing her memory, she would just vegetate in a home. We cannot see her suffer like this; she cannot see herself suffer like this.

We stayed till she fell asleep then left to go home, none of us speaking on the way home, just in a complete daze.

Keeping up a brave face

11th December: We all are making sure that we keep the atmosphere lively when we see mum, she must not suspect anything. We just want her to be happy but it's so hard keeping up a brave face.

Hand painful

12th December: Mum was very calm tonight. It seems that when she was on dialysis she was more confused. Her good hand is now very painful and she is quite uncomfortable with it. We will see if they can give mum anything to help the pain.

Every night now all three of us go to the hospital together. My niece also came tonight and mum is very happy just watching all of us talk together. Her hand is still painful but she seems to know that she is in hospital now even though she doesn't actually say so. I wonder who is protecting who?

Liquid morphine for the pain

13th December: The palliative care team from the hospital have been visiting Mum. Palliative care is specialized medical care for people with serious illnesses. It is focused on providing patients with relief from the symptoms, pain, and stress of a serious illness whatever the prognosis. Their goal is to improve quality of life for both the patient and the family.

I telephoned them today and spoke to Alice, one of the specialist sisters who has been seeing mum. She said they work closely with the doctors and make sure that mum is comfortable. Apparently, she is going to prescribe a very mild liquid morphine medicine for her that will help kill the pain especially when she has to be moved in bed. She was very kind and said that if I needed to ask anything I can always phone. She will keep me up to date on any new developments concerning mum.

Mum was more confused again tonight. Her hand was hurting a lot and the nurse gave her an injection for the pain; thankfully, it worked quite quickly.

Alert

14th December: Mum was very alert today. She seemed really good and not too confused. She had some food and we had a lovely chat talking about my boys and my dog Max. She really loves my dog (a yellow Labrador). Every Saturday I used to do mums shopping and then spend the day with her. I would always bring Max with me over to mum and mum would have some nice tip bits waiting for him. When I used to say let's go to nanny now he would run to the door in excitement.

Sleeping more

15th December: Mum has slept all day today, she didn't want any breakfast or lunch and when I got to the hospital at 5.30 to take over from my sister mum was still sleeping. I kissed her head and she opened her eyes, she looked up at me smiled and then closed her eyes again. She was in a very contented sleep, I left about 9 o'clock. I phoned the hospital an hour later to see how she was and she was still sleeping.

Did we laugh

16th December: My two best friends came to see mum today Marsha and Jackie, she was really happy to see them. We all go back a long time together, over 50 years. But the funniest thing was that she thought Jackie was Marsha's mother. Oh did we laugh; Jackie will never live that one down.
We were all chatting and laughing a lot amongst ourselves and mum was looking at us smiling, she just loves to listen to us all talking. She looks quite good and I keep on wondering maybe her kidneys will kick in on their own accord now she is off the dialysis. Can you imagine?

Give her the world

17th December: Another good night, mum is enjoying eating a nice slice of cheese with her Guinness. We are now giving her anything she wants; whatever she fancies, I would give her the world if I could.

Irritable

18th December: Tonight Mum was very irritable; she seems to have a cold and didn't want the nurses to wash her, she also did not want to take any painkillers. We asked the nurse to come and wash mum and when they had finished we persuaded mum to have the painkillers.

Mum eventually settled down and by 9pm had fallen asleep so we left.
Looking pasty

19th December: Mum was better in herself today, but her hands are still so very bad and hurting her even though she is having painkillers to help. Mum's face colour seems a bit pasty; it must be because her kidneys aren't working properly. The Matron rang me to see when we could speak so I have arranged to see her at 5.30 tomorrow.

The truth is starting to come out

20th December: Lindy, Mum's nurse for the day telephoned me and said that Mum is asking for a Guinness but they don't have any left, so she asked if I could bring some tonight. Shortly afterwards she telephoned me again to say that Mum is now saying that she wants some cheese. Lindy said Mum is so very funny today and in good spirits, all the nurses are laughing at Mum's request.
I had the meeting with the Matron this afternoon. I thought it was going to be about Mum's condition, but she wanted to talk about the formal complaint that I sent into the hospital.
She said that she felt that Mum's blood should have been checked more frequently in the first few weeks, but there was quite a young team on the ward, that's no excuse. The painkillers that Mum had been given would never have been given to anyone with any kind of kidney problem, and on Mum's notes she mentioned that in 2006 some kind of abnormality was indicated. However, she went on to say that even if Mum had not been given the painkillers there still might have been complications. I acknowledged there is always an element of risk with any surgery, but Mum was never given the chance to find out.

She asked if we could have a meeting with Mum's specialist Mr Shah in the New Year and if we would like her to attend the meeting. I said yes as it would be very helpful especially as she is on the renal ward and Mr Shah is on orthopaedics. I thanked her very much for her support.

I went in to see mum after our meeting and she was quite happy but she looked even frailer than she had been. Later on my sisters came. She enjoys seeing all of us together and also mentioned to us that it will soon be Christmas. She said that we must put the lottery on and gave me her numbers.

Seems to know

21st December - 22nd December: Mum is very depressed but more compos mentis than she has been for a while. She seems to know how ill she is even though she isn't saying anything to us. Quite often she looks right into my eyes but without saying anything, it's as if she's talking to me with her eyes, piercing through me.
She has been sleeping for most of the time and I have told the nursing staff to be aware that she seems to be getting depressed again.

Which light should I go to?

23rd December: Today Mum was sleeping the whole time while my sister was there, when my other sister and I arrived late afternoon she was with the nursing staff having her sores cleaned and dressed. She was quite stressed but she eventually calmed down and we made her as comfortable as we could. Mum couldn't stop staring at my sister, I said, "Penny for your thoughts, Mum."

She said, "I don't know which light to go to."

I replied, "You'll know eventually, Mum, which light to go to."

Mum fell asleep about 7.30 and looked very contented. I

wonder if she saw a light.

At least it's now the Christmas holidays and my sisters and I are not working till the beginning of January so we can spend more time with mum. She really has not got long to live and we really want to spend as much time as possible with her. We cannot comprehend this is happening, it's like a bad dream.

Still holding her own

24th December: Mum is still holding her own but is now very depressed. I really think that she has had enough, she is quite irritable and not really wanting to talk, I think that she just wants to go to sleep and not wake up. She is in pain but will not take the painkillers from the nurses; she only takes them if my sisters or I give them to her. How we hate to see her suffer like this.

Christmas Day

25th December: When I arrived at the hospital Mum was not good, she was very depressed again and did not want to talk to my sisters and I. Mum had refused the medication from the nurses so I tried to give it to her. She really did not want to know and told me to go away. I told her how important it was that she had the painkillers. I said, "If I was in that bed and you were sitting on this chair you would be telling me to have the medication, you would not want me to be in pain mum would you? She looked at me and without saying anything took the pills.

After about half an hour mum became more like herself and asked me for some tea. The painkillers must of started to kick in which must be making her feel better and with my sisters we all had tea together.

I brought mum a lovely Amethyst bracelet for Christmas and put it on her wrist. Amethyst has healing qualities, well it can't hurt. How much longer can mum go on for without her kidneys working?

Skin really irritating

26th December: Mum is pretty much the same, but her skin was irritating her terribly today. Oh no, I thought, not again and this time it cannot be from the dialysis. My sister was scratching her back and I was scratching her tummy. I asked the nurse to give mum some antihistamines which seemed to help.
Mum then said to me and my sister, "Go to bed both of you, you have work tomorrow." Mum must have thought we were at home and had gone back in time again.
We did not leave the hospital late as mum just wanted to sleep.

I love you

27th December: I really don't think that it will be long now. Mum has been sleeping a lot today. When I arrived, she looked in a daze. I said, "I love you, Mum."

She replied, "I love you too." but in a very weak voice. I gave her something to eat but then she said she felt itchy again and wanted me to scratch her back. I gave her an antihistamine tablet to help her itchy dry skin and then she fell asleep. I hope she sleeps well tonight.

Thought she would have gone a week ago

28th December: Again Mum has been sleeping most of the day and when she opens her eyes she really doesn't want to talk. I was there with my sister in the afternoon and my other sister came in the evening so I left. My sister told me that mum woke up later and said she was quite awake but not talking, what a difference to earlier on in the day. The nurse told my sister that she would have thought mum would have gone a week ago and she is amazed mum is still here. She sure is a strong lady! Seems like she is holding on just for my sisters and I.

Deteriorating

29th December: Mum is deteriorating a lot now. She is so weak and doesn't have any energy to talk but she's quite alert and awake. This evening she was very aggravated and throwing the bed covers off of her. Eventually I calmed her down with some gentle massaging, I was gently stroking her body very lightly which seemed to relax her. She then looked at me and started to smile, something that she has not done for quite a few days, she then went into a lovely peaceful sleep.

Wants to be left alone

30th December: Mum just wants to be left alone this morning, she won't allow the nurses to wash her and she does not want to eat anything. Mum had half a cup of tea at lunchtime then went to sleep. She is still sleeping tonight, but did open her eyes for a moment and gave my sisters a lovely smile then went back to sleep.

Never going home

31st December: Mum was lovely today, it's New Years Eve and I got to the hospital just after midday. She was awake and even though she seemed dazed I could communicate with her. We even had a little bit of a laugh as weak as she was and I was talking about the old times. Times when we all used to go out for a drive in the country with daddy and my aunt and uncle when I was little picking bluebells in the forest. Times when mum made her lovely Sunday roast and we would then all listen to Billy Cottons Big Band Show on the radiogram. Times when we would drive to the coast and walk on the beach especially when dad fell down a hole in the sand, he was so accident prone, oh did we laugh.

I left the hospital at 5.30 when my sisters came.

I spent New Year's evening at my cousin Joceyne's. I could not believe that six months had passed since mum first went into hospital.

How were we ever to know that on that wonderful hot summer's night in July when my mother took me and my sisters out for dinner the day before she went into hospital she would never be coming home.

We were sitting in the glorious sunshine laughing and planning what we would be doing once she could walk properly again.

It breaks my heart that our mother will never again feel the sun on her face, she will never again be going back to her home, she will never again go to the shops, she will never again get in her car and drive, she will never, never, never again do anything with us ever again.

Male nurse just walked away

1st January 2008

When I arrived at the hospital on New Year's Day Mum was sleeping. She didn't look good at all, she was breathing quite heavy and her skin colour was quite grey. The nurses came in to wash her and then she perked up. She started to look much better when some colour came back to her face. I gave her some salmon salad and she said she also wanted some fruit. She then said, "I'm going to be sick." She started to vomit. I did not know which way to turn, what to grab first.

I ran outside the room and the male nurse in charge of mum today was standing at the nurses' station, I was shouting to him that my mother had been sick, help me, help me my mother's being sick! He gave me a bowl then just walked away. I ran back to mum with the bowl. I carried on shouting for a nurse to come in the room. How could I leave her? Mum had vomit all down her front. I took a towel and placed it on mum's chest and finally went back outside. I saw the male nurse and shouted, "Are you coming in to see to my mother?" He replied, "I'm doing something." I was so angry but did not have the time to fight with him. I ran back to mum and tried to clean her up as best as I could then finally another nurse came in to help.

When mum was cleaned up she looked a lot better. I was making her smile and we had a cuddle. When my sisters came mum was quite funny and her personality returned. Mum finally went off to sleep about 7.30. Hopefully she'll have a good sleep.

I complained to the staff nurse about the male nurse and said, "I know you're short staffed but you can't leave my mother like this. She should not be treated like this, no one should" She admitted that even though they were short staffed this shouldn't have happened and she would have a word with the male nurse.

What on earth would have happened if I hadn't have been there? My mother only has a short time left; how can that nurse be so callous?

Been off of dialyses for 21 days

2nd January: It's been 21 days since Mum was taken off the dialyses machine. My sister went to see mum this afternoon and found her sleeping. When I arrived with my other sister mum was just waking up. She seemed in a bit of a daze when we arrived but she managed half a cup of tea but didn't want anything to eat. We had a little chat then she went off to sleep again.

Chapter Seven

Six Months in hospital

3rd January: I am back to work now, I rang to see how mum was today and the nurse said she had some tea and at lunchtime had a little food. When I arrived at the hospital tonight mum was awake but looked dazed again, I think she may have just woken up. She looked at me as if she didn't recognise me but she was smiling. I kissed her and said, "Hello, Mum" then told her that my boys and Max my dog sends her a big kiss. Well I said Max sends a big lick. She smiled and seemed to come too. She remarked on my top that I was wearing being too small (it had shrunk in the wash). So I said "typical of me to shrink something".

We had a cuddle then she said to me, "I'm getting old Jo."

I was taken aback and said "but mum so am I, we're both getting older." She repeated to me she was getting old.

I said "Mum, wherever we are we will always be together, no matter how old we both get.

She smiled and said, "You're marvellous."

The tears just started coming out of my eyes. "You're marvellous mum," She then said, "Give me a kiss goodnight."

I bent down and I gave her such a beautiful kiss with the tears running down my face. She then closed her eyes and went to sleep. I sat down and just stared into thin air thinking how lucky am I to capture all these last few days with my mum. How lucky are we to share all the memories together.

When my sisters came mum woke up for a while then while I was stroking her face she went back into a peaceful sleep.

Thumbs up

4th January: The nurse said that this morning mum had refused breakfast and any medication; it seems that mum's attitude depends on who is the assigned nurse of the day. She seems to have her favourite ones and had a lovely female nurse yesterday but she doesn't like the male nurses.

Mum was not good tonight. She was talking very quietly but I couldn't understand what she was saying. I put my ear close to her mouth and she was moving her lips but I really didn't know what she was saying. When my son Darren came in to the room mum's face lit up and as usual and she gave him a lovely smile. Darren puts his thumb up to mum and says, "Alright, Mench." They always have had this warm gesture together when they see each other and mum always replies by putting her thumb up to Darren.

Well as weak as she is mum very very slowly slightly raised her hand and very slowly lifted her thumb. We all could not believe it, she still was here with us, she still knew what she was doing and it was this love that was keeping her going.

Sore throat

5th January: Mum is complaining of a sore throat today. She also has a headache. She can hardly talk again; it was so hard to hear her. I only hope that she is not coming down with a cold.

Jo let me go

6th January: It's Sunday and I arrived at the hospital about 2.30. Mum didn't look good. She had a very chesty cough and couldn't keep any fluids down. I tried to give her some painkillers but she couldn't take it. She was trying to talk to me but I couldn't understand what she was saying. I put my ear to her mouth and then in quite a clear voice mum said, "Jo, let me go."

My heart sank, and I said "I am letting you go, mum, please don't worry, we will all be fine." Mum didn't reply just closed her eyes. When my sisters arrived mum woke up and we tried to give her some soup but she was too chesty. I called the nurse and she gave mum a nebuliser which is to help her chest. A face mask is put over the nose and mouth which sprays a fine mist of medication to help you breath, but mum was uncomfortable with it and would not have it on her face.

Mum started to relax then said to me very quietly, "You look just like me." (Well I do resemble her)

I said yes I do, but you're more beautiful. She finally went to sleep about 7.30. I hope she sleeps peacefully tonight.

Kiss

7th January: I phoned the hospital this morning and mums nurse for the day Jane said she is fine and has had a wash. My sister phoned me shortly after arriving at the hospital this afternoon and gave me a slightly different story. Mum's breathing was very bad and she was sleeping all the time. I arrived at the hospital about 6 o' clock after work and mum was still sleeping. She woke up after I had been there for about an hour and she was trying to say something but she was so weak she didn't have the strength to speak. I put my ear to her lips and it sounded like mum was trying to say kiss. She then made a kiss movement with her lips. I put my face to her lips and very gently mum placed her lips touching my cheek and she kissed me. I will always remember that kiss until the day I die.

Mum was lying on her back not having the energy to move but kept on opening her eyes to look at us all then closing them and then opening her eyes again as if to check that we were still there. At one stage mum even appeared to smile at us. My other sister arrived and I think Mum tried to say her name but the words just would not come out. I just kept on lightly stroking mums face, which seemed to comfort her. She went to sleep about 9 o'clock so we left. Sleep well, my darling Mother.

Goodbye my darling, till we meet again

8th January 2008: Today is no different to any other day. I woke up at 6.30 and as usual had a shower, made breakfast, took my dog out for his morning walk then got in my car and drove to work.

My sister wasn't working today so she was going to the hospital about 12 o'clock. I was quite busy at work but I could not really concentrate on anything. At about three in the afternoon my sister rang me on my mobile phone to say that Mum's breathing is really getting bad and she thinks that I should come to the hospital straight away. I told my boss Steven that I must leave straight away to go to the hospital as mum seems to be getting worse. He said no problem go, go. Do you want me to drive you? I told him that wasn't necessary and ran to my car. The journey to the hospital takes about half an hour and it was the longest half an hour I have ever had. All the time while driving in my car I'm praying please dear god please don't let mum pass away before I have had time to say goodbye.

The parking at the hospital is always very bad and you can be waiting for ages to park. As I was approaching the hospital I'm thinking please let there be a parking space. As I got to the car park someone was just pulling out of a space and I drove right into it and parked. It was as if someone was really looking out for me.

I ran as fast as I could to get to mum. When I got to mum's room she was breathing very badly and she was gasping for breath. I quickly phoned my other sister and said get here as quick as you can, leave now. There was no nurse in with mum just my sister so I went outside to find someone. A team of doctors, one of whom was Dr Smith, were walking round the wards. I shouted, "My mother is really bad, she cannot breathe!"

Dr Smith replied, "We are just doing our rounds and will be in soon." I shouted with tears in my eyes, "She is dying, please come!"

A doctor came in straight away and said he would give mum an injection to help her breathe better and make her comfortable. He asked if we would be staying and I said, "All night." My other sister arrived with the same look of bewilderment as we had. It was as if this was a bad dream, how could this be the end.

My sisters and I sat round Mum's bed. I stood up and was gently stroking mum's face. I said, "Its okay, Mum, you can go now, we'll be alright." Mum's breathing started to get slower and slower but she seemed to be fighting it. I carried on stroking her face very gently and talking softly telling her how much we all loved her.

Our mother took one more final breath and passed away at 6.15.

Goodbye my darling, till we meet again.

Chapter 8

Conclusion

The Letter from the hospital dated 23rd January 2008

The actual letter from the hospital sent to me after my mother had passed away.
I have drawn attention to key phrases by using bold lettering

Dear Mrs Slater

Thank you for your e-mail dated 2 November 2007 about the care your late mother, received at our Hospital following her admission on 19 July 2007. Please accept our profound and unreserved apologies for the upset and distress caused and for the delay in replying to you. **As your mother was an inpatient, it was not possible to remove her medical notes from the ward to enable us to investigate the concerns raised in your letter.** I would also like to extend to you and your family my condolences on the recent sad loss of your mother.

You have asked us to address a number of questions, namely:

1. How could your mothers hip dislocate days after the operation?
2. Why did your mother wait one and a half weeks for an x-ray?
3. Why was a saline drip administered even though doctors noted that too much fluid had already been administered?
4. Additionally, you believe that the use of painkillers affected your mother's kidneys.

The investigation into your concerns has been co-ordinated by our senior complaints manager - surgery, anaesthetics and critical care directorate and overseen by the general manager - surgery, anaesthetics and critical care directorate and is now complete. Mr Shah consultant orthopaedic surgeon, has contributed information to our investigation. I understand that in 1990 your mother underwent surgery to replace her right hip and further remedial surgery following complications. Unfortunately, in 2003, your mother fell and fractured (broke) her right ankle and this injury required surgical intervention. Additionally, as a result of this injury, your mother developed intermittent problems with her right hip, which dislocated two years ago when your mother was getting out of a car. Your mother went on to dislocate her hip on three subsequent occasions, i.e., 20 April 2006, 26 April 2006 and on 24 December 2006 when she also injured her upper arm. In light of these recurrent dislocations, doctors sought advice from Mr Shah, who has a particular interest in orthopaedic hip conditions.

Mr Shah reviewed your mother in his private patients' clinic on 30 April 2007 and at his NHS clinic on 3 May 2007. Following these appointments, Mr Shah added your mother's name to the waiting list for revision surgery of her right hip, which we carried out on 20 July 2007. Mr Shah tells me that the surgery proceeded uneventfully **but post-operative blood tests and previous blood tests showed abnormal kidney function dating back to 2006 and abnormal urea and electrolytes levels (essential chemicals in the body). Unfortunately, junior medical staff did not bring the results of the post-operative blood tests to the attention of Mr Shah who has brought this unfortunate lapse in communication to the attention of junior doctors to avoid a recurrence.**

Your mother experienced some discomfort in the days following her operation, however an x-ray performed on 23 July confirmed that the hip was in a satisfactory position. Physiotherapists worked with your mother to improve her mobility and Mr Shah's team reviewed your mother on a daily basis. It seems that your mother showed no clinical signs of a dislocated hip, *however it appears that doctors did not fully appreciate the pain and discomfort your mother experienced.* Mr Shah reviewed your mother on 2 August and he was concerned that your mother was finding it difficult to mobilise and therefore requested an x-ray of her right hip. The x-ray showed that your mother's right hip had again, dislocated and Mr Shah decided to take your mother to theatre and examine the affected hip under anaesthetic.

In preparing your mother for this further surgery, doctors performed routine blood tests, which again showed abnormal kidney function. As soon as the orthopaedic team noted the abnormal blood results they asked their nephrology colleagues (specialists in kidney conditions) to review your mother. The orthopaedic team advised the nephrologists of the importance of operating on your mother's hip at the earliest opportunity. However, the first priority was for the nephrologists to stabilise your mother before taking her to theatre and I understand this occurred on 11 August.

Mr Shah tells me that in relation to the fluid therapy given to your mother, the nephrologists directed this aspect of your mother's care and members of the orthopaedic team discussed this with their nephrology colleagues before prescribing intravenous fluids.

I understand that patients like your mother, who have a history of recurrent dislocations of the hip and undergo revision surgery, have a particularly high rate of further dislocation. *In addition, your mother's kidney function deteriorated following surgery. This may have been in part due to the effect major surgery has on patients or possibly due to the few doses of non-steroidal anti-*

inflammatory medication your mother received post-operatively. Doctors prescribed this medication, which together with the recent operation and pre-existing kidney problems may have lead to the significant deterioration in her kidney function.
At this stage I feel, it is important to express our apologies for the delay in responding to your letter of complaint. In order to investigate any complaint, it is essential that those involved in the investigation, have full access to the relevant case notes. **As your mother was an inpatient, it was not appropriate to remove her notes from the ward to conduct an investigation.** However, as a trust we are keen to ensure that we deal with any complaints or concerns raised by patients or their relatives in an appropriate and timely fashion. It is clear that our handling of this complaint was slow and for this, we are extremely sorry. However, as a result of this complaint, we have reviewed our procedures. If we now receive any complaints that relate to patients who are currently inpatients, we will in the first instance ask our matrons to liaise with the patient and their family to see if we can answer their questions and go some way to addressing their concerns if it is not possible to conduct a full investigation at that time.

All concerned in your late mother's care were extremely sorry to learn that she passed away on 8 January and send their condolences to you and your family.

There is no doubt that we owe you our profound and unreserved apologies for the upset and distress caused. If I, or any member of my staff, can be of assistance to you please do not hesitate to contact us.

Yours sincerely

Mary Darlington

A message from Joanna

I wish that my mother was still here and had never gone into hospital for that fatal hip operation. I wish that I had never had to write this book and I wish that I could turn back the clock, but alas that is not possible.
Sometimes in adversity we find our life's purpose.

My blog www.thelastsixmonths.co.uk was started because of all the letters and emails of support sent to me when extracts of my mother's story was published in The Mail on Sunday in June 2011.
I never expected the reaction I received from people all over the UK

telling me of their own horrendous stories of loved ones in hospital. I decided to publish them on my blog as it seemed that The Last Six Months had given people a voice to be heard.

There had to be a reason why I was put in this position to capture the last six months of my mother's life so I decided in September 2011 to go back to my diary and tell the whole story in a book hoping that a wider coverage would have an even greater impact to those who govern this country and for once will listen to us the people.

I am one of many amongst a magnitude of people fighting for the right for people to be treated with respect, dignity and ultimate care within our NHS system.

We have many dedicated doctors and nurses working in our hospitals of which the bad apples tarnish the excellent work they do. They are also frustrated with the NHS system which is out of their control.

The NHS has to change and has to change now.

Let's hope the fight has begun.

If you have a story to tell please email me
Email: thelast6months@hotmail.co.uk

© Joanna Slater 2010